Growing Under Glass

Your Guide to Greenhouse Gardening Success

by Hilery Hixon

Growing Under Glass:
Your Guide to Greenhouse Gardening Success
www.growingunderglass.com

BookSurge Publishing
Charleston, South Carolina
1-866-308-6235

Book Design by Graphic Web Design
A Division of Crazy Dog Publications

Library of Congress Control Number: 2009902636

ISBN: 1-4392-3315-2
EAN: 9781439233153

Printed in the United States of America

Dedication:

To Adem, my dear husband who believed in me.

To my husband's parents who supported me throughout the process of writing this book.

And to my mother and father for giving me the corner in the yard to grow my heart's desire that started it all.

Contents

Deciding What to Grow Under Glass 71

Life in the Greenhouse 93

Resources 95

Index 102

Introduction

Most of us got hooked on gardening when we were kids. We experienced the wonder of nurturing a seed and watching it grow and change day by day. Growing up, I always had my own corner of the garden to plant whatever my heart desired and I took great pride in my okra plants.

When I was in first grade, our class conducted a science experiment. On a Monday, each of us was given a lima bean. We moistened a paper towel, folded the lima bean inside, sealed the paper towel in a plastic bag and pinned the bag on a bulletin board next to our each of our names. On Friday, we opened the bags and gasped in amazement when we found our lima beans had germinated! I still experience the same wonder every time I start new plants from seed in my greenhouse.

My greenhouse began as an experiment. As a hobby gardener, could I really pull off a greenhouse in the desert southwest? I am not a botanist, a horticulturist or a master gardener, but I was determined to find as much information as possible about growing under glass.

What I found is there is a lot of literature on gardening and on greenhouse construction, however not as much on the actual process of what goes on inside the greenhouse, and even less about greenhouse gardening in desert climates. This spawned the project of writing, compiling and sharing information about growing a productive garden indoors.

After your greenhouse is built, there are a multitude of decisions to make. This book is divided into four sections to help guide you along the way:
- The Greenhouse Structure
- Growing Guidelines
- Deciding What to Grow Under Glass
- Resources

Arm yourself with as much information as possible, take the process step-by-step and most of all have fun! Experience is the best teacher; learn to trust your instincts. Your plants will tell you when they need help or when they are happy. A greenhouse is a commitment, and with that commitment, your greenhouse will reward you with a year-round growing season.

Gardening is an adventure, so get out to your greenhouse and starting growing!

The Greenhouse Structure

The greenhouse structure is an important thing; it is what keeps regulated temperature in and the elements out. Since you have picked up this book, you most likely already have your greenhouse built. If your greenhouse is not yet built, I commend you on taking the steps to educate yourself on everything that goes into maintaining and operating a hobby greenhouse.

First off, check the stability of the structure. Are any sections of the greenhouse shaky? Do they need reinforcement? If the greenhouse is not new, do any repairs need to be made and do any cracks need sealed up? Is the roof solid? In regions where it snows, the roof needs to be able to handle the weight of the snow if the pitch of the roof is not steep enough to shed the snow. It is easier to take care of these things now before plants are moved inside.

The first greenhouse I built was from an inexpensive kit. While kit greenhouses are fine for most applications, my husband and I live in an open, windy area. The kit I purchased did not show a wind rating. The first windstorm we experienced, the roof sheared right off the greenhouse. It was not even standing for a week!

If you have not built your greenhouse yet are looking into a kit greenhouse, call the manufacturer and ask questions to make sure that your greenhouse will work for your location and your application. Ask for a wind rating. In northern areas, make sure the roof will hold the weight of snow. In southern areas, make sure the glazing is properly treated with a UV coating that can withstand the harsh sun of your region. If the manufacturer cannot answer these questions, it may be prudent to look into a different greenhouse.

Greenhouse Maintenance

A greenhouse is an investment in money and time. Even though the primary focus of the greenhouse is the plants inside, it is important to keep the structure in the forefront of your mind. Maintaining your structure will ensure many years of indoor gardening enjoyment.

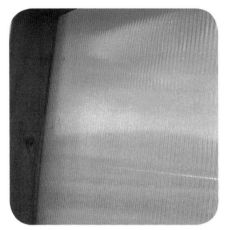

Polycarbonate Glazing

Glazing

Glazing is a fancy name for the material of the "windows" of the greenhouse. Light enters the greenhouse through the glazing. Keeping the glazing clean is important for your plants to get the sunlight they need. Make a habit of checking the glazing on a weekly basis to see if it needs to be cleaned.

If your glazing is polycarbonate or glass, check the edges once a year to see if it needs to be resealed. Sealing is easy with a tube of silicone, but before you lay down a new bead of silicone, peel up the damaged or dried out silicone first.

Glass will last a long time, however it is fragile when it comes to impact. Polycarbonate is more durable, yet tends to yellow over time and may need to be replaced after ten years.

With polyethylene (plastic film) glazing, check the surface once a week for tears and repair accordingly. Be prepared for the need to replace the polyethylene once a year as twelve months of wind, rain and possibly hail quickly takes its toll. Make sure the edges are secured so the wind cannot get underneath. If the wind can pick up the edges, you can be almost guaranteed that the wind will tear it up quickly. Visit your local nursery during the winter months to check out their temporary greenhouse setup and you will see exactly what I mean. Polyethylene is less expensive than glass and polycarbonate, but it is much less durable.

Polyethylene Damage

Green Thumb: Check plastic sheeting daily during extreme temperatures as tears will let out regulated air. A hole could spell greenhouse disaster!

Framing

Framing is often overlooked during maintenance, yet it is the most important part of the maintenance process as the framing is what holds up the greenhouse!

Resin and aluminum require virtually no maintenance, just an occasional looking over to inspect for cracks or wear and tear. Aluminum does corrode quickly when in contact with high concentrations of copper. As a consequence, do not allow it to come into contact with pressure-treated wood.

Greenhouse with Wooden Structural Support

In the Greenhouse

For my wood structure greenhouse, I painted the exposed wood. Since my north wall is an insulated wall without glazing, the white paint reflects more light back into the space. At first, I wondered if it was going to make a difference with the light reflection. Before I painted the wall, there was light in the greenhouse. After I painted the wall, it was bright in the greenhouse!

Maintaining a wooden structure requires a little more work as exposure to high amounts of moisture promotes rot. The quandary here is that most moisture treatments contain chemicals harmful to plants. Should condensation from the treated wood drip on the plants, the plants could die. If you are growing food crops inside your greenhouse, make sure your lumber is not treated with arsenate. There are numerous organic treatments as alternatives to the traditional wood treatments.

Flooring

While flooring does not require much in the way of maintenance, there are important considerations for each of the flooring options. No matter your material choice, it is important to have adequate drainage.

Mulch

I have read a lot of mixed opinions about mulch. It is inexpensive and easy to replace, however I have also seen people mention that it attracts insects. In the desert southwest, bark chips are among the favorite hiding spots for scorpions!

Mulch will also break down and need to be replaced periodically. Another issue is that some kinds of mulch do not compact well, leading to an uneven floor surface and wobbly benches.

Concrete Slab

A concrete slab is the most expensive option and provides a very solid base. For those that require wheelchair accessibility, concrete is definitely the way to go.

The issue with a concrete slab is that there is limited drainage and may be slippery when wet. If you do not have a floor drain inside your greenhouse, examine your conditions and if you have drainage issues, consult a contractor.

Gravel

Washed three-quarter inch gravel is available for purchase from nearly all rock yards and it is not as expensive as you would think! It is great for holding moisture after watering it down to increase the humidity in your greenhouse. Its shape also lends to a stable surface for benches to rest upon.

Gravel Floor with Paving Stones

Paving Stones

You can place down paving stones to give your greenhouse a flat "floor". They have a nice outdoor look to them and are available in a wide range of colors and styles. Prices vary greatly upon those options.

Types of Greenhouses

The first decision to make is to decide what type of greenhouse you want. This can depend on the plants you intend to grow and what your budget is for maintaining a greenhouse. It is important to look into the expenses of keeping the greenhouse going, as some types require more monetary investment than others.

Each type of greenhouse refers to the temperature maintained inside. The size of the greenhouse will also directly affect the cost of the climate control; a small greenhouse will cost less to heat than a large greenhouse. Also take into account your region. In a cold northern region, it will take more resources to keep a greenhouse heated than in a warmer southern region.

Let's take a look at the different types of greenhouses.

Hot Greenhouse

The temperature in a hot greenhouse is maintained above sixty-five degrees. Typically a hot greenhouse is used to grow tropical and exotic plants, including orchids. These types of greenhouses will most likely require a heater.

Warm Greenhouse

A warm greenhouse maintains a temperature above fifty-five degrees. Many plants are perfectly suited to a warm greenhouse, such as would be used in an outdoor garden. In northern regions, additional heating may still be required.

Cool Greenhouse

In a cool greenhouse, temperatures dip down to forty degrees. It is still frost-free, which is great for overwintering container plants and bulbs that do not need warmer temperatures to survive.

Ranunculus Bulbs

Water & Electricity

If your greenhouse does not already have water and electricity, this is a good time to consider having these two services run to your greenhouse.

Should you not have a water spigot next to or inside the greenhouse, having a water line run definitely makes life easier. Imagine carrying buckets of water back and forth to water your plants! In my greenhouse, I have a water pipe coming up out of the floor in the corner with a spigot on top. This provides me with all the water I need and also makes the line available for future additions to the space, including a sink.

For those on well water, I highly recommend an in-line filter. The filter will remove a lot of the minerals from the water that build up on water wands and misters. By removing these minerals, the life of your watering accessories will be greatly extended.

While water at the greenhouse is a necessity, electricity is more of a luxury. Lighting, grow lamps and fans use electricity. Unless you use solar panels, these accessories require electrical to be run to the structure. In warmer regions, a fan will be needed to help regulate the temperature otherwise it will get so hot inside the greenhouse during the summer that you will cook your plants.

Since there is a lot of moisture in the greenhouse, I recommend a professional wire the electrical system to make sure everything is watertight and does not cause a fire hazard. I have a moisture-proof light, covered electrical outlet and the wiring for my ventilation fan is sealed.

Regulating Temperatures

Unless you use your greenhouse solely for overwintering plants, measures will need to be taken to regulate the temperature inside. Without intervention, the nighttime temperature inside during the winter may only be a few degrees warmer than the outside temperature, and in the summer (especially in hot, sunny regions) the daytime temperature inside could be twenty to thirty degrees hotter than outside. When my greenhouse first went up, before I put the temperature regulation measures in place, the temperature inside climbed to over one hundred twenty five degrees!

I highly recommend going through a summer and winter season prior to introducing expensive and highly temperature sensitive plants into the greenhouse. This enables you to adjust and perfect the methods you use to keep your greenhouse temperature warm and cool.

Keep in mind that what is comfortable for a plant is not always comfortable for a human, so heat and cool only to what your plants require. Wind chill and heat index are measures of what temperature feels like to the skin and is not a measure of temperature for plants.

Cooling Hot Conditions

In cooler regions, a window vent opened at the top of the greenhouse is sufficient to keep the greenhouse usable in the summertime. In warmer regions, more intervention is required.

Ventilation

Using ventilation can do wonders for cooling temperatures inside the greenhouse. A window vent located at the top can be opened to release the heat. Since the nature of heat is to rise, this window vent at the crest of the greenhouse will let the heat out. Automatic vent openers can be purchased to open the window vent as the temperature inside rises.

For more aggressive ventilation, a vent and fan system will more actively transfer heat out of the greenhouse. With ventilation fans, it is more efficient to "pull" the air instead of "push" it. Therefore, the ideal location for a ventilation fan is on the west wall at the crest. Since the fan is located at a high point, they do not work well in conjunction with roof vents. The fan will pull hot air from the roof vent instead of cooler air from the air intake.

Here in the northern hemisphere of the planet, greenhouses are oriented with one long side receiving southern exposure for maximum sunlight inside. (For those in the southern hemisphere, the opposite is true.) The morning sun on the east side of the greenhouse is cooler than the afternoon sun on the west side of the greenhouse.

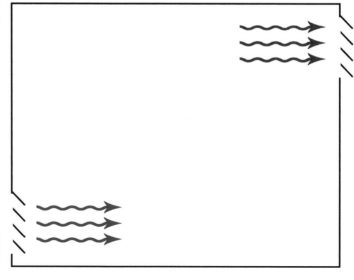

Cool Air Intake and
Hot Air Exhaust

With the fan on the west wall, the fan will pull the hot air out of the greenhouse. The ideal location for the air intake is low to the ground on the east wall. Cooler air pulled from the east side of the greenhouse will replace the hot air pulled out by the ventilation fan.

Louvers and shutters are available to place over the air intake to seal off the vent when the fan is not in use. I also recommend a screen be placed over the intake vent to prevent insects access to the greenhouse.

There are a multitude of options for ventilation fans. Greenhouse supply shops offer several different sizes of fans with built-in shutters to keep bugs out while the fan is not running. Home improvement stores sell gable attic fans that work quite well for a greenhouse application. Some fans are noisier than others, so if the sound produced by the fan is an issue, check the store's return policy before you purchase just in case the sound is a problem.

**Attic Fan Used
For Ventilation**

Green Thumb: The most important thing to look for when selecting a fan is the CFM rating.

Exhaust Shutter

CFM represents the cubic feet per minute of air that the fan circulates out of a given area. The fan's packaging provides this information. In the resources section of this book, there is a website address that will help you to select what size fan and air intake is needed for your size of greenhouse. Also useful is a thermostat so the fan turns on and off at a given temperature. Most attic fans come with a thermostatic control, however most greenhouse fans do not, so the control will need to be purchased separately.

Shade

Sometimes ventilation is just not enough and shade will need to be introduced. Here in the southwest United States, a shade cloth is a necessity during the summer.

Amazingly, there is a large selection of shade cloths available at the home improvement stores and greenhouse supply shops based on how much light needs to be allowed through the cloth. There are even reflective shade cloths that reflect heat out yet still allow light through.

Although the shade cloth can be hung inside along the ceiling, it is more effective when attached outside to the roof. When it is placed inside, the sun will still heat the air inside the greenhouse. In windy locations, a shade cloth outside the greenhouse can be an issue. Make sure to securely attach it to the roof and if necessary, build a frame for the shade cloth so the edges cannot be picked up by the wind.

With a little planning, nature can provide shade for you. If a deciduous tree is located on the south side of the greenhouse, it will provide shade in the summertime and allow light through to the greenhouse when it sheds its leaves in the wintertime. Tall annual plants, such as sunflowers, can also be used outside the south wall for summer shade.

Humidity

In very hot locations, shade and ventilation is still not enough and humidity needs to be introduced. Spraying the floor with water is a quick fix to drop the temperature a couple of degrees. As the water evaporates, it helps cool the air. Many plants even appreciate the extra humidity, especially tropical plants.

A misting system hooked up a timer to run during the hottest part of the day will cool the air significantly. Typical systems cool the air around ten to fifteen degrees, however more sophisticated systems can cool the air by as much as thirty degrees. There are even fogging systems that are a bit pricey, however in hot, dry conditions, the cooling effect is dramatic.

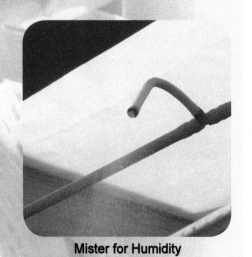

Shade Cloth

Mister for Humidity and Cooling

Misting nozzles can clog very easily. When purchasing your misting system, get a filter that goes in-line from the water spigot. This will reduce the mineral build-up on the nozzles, but not eliminate it completely. Once the nozzles start to clog, remove them, put them in a water bottle with white vinegar, and shake vigorously. Wash the nozzles off and put them back on the system. I keep a spare set on hand just for this purpose so the system is not inactive during the cleaning process. Cleaning your nozzles will greatly extend the life of the mist system, however be prepared to periodically replace the nozzles.

Evaporative Cooling

Sometimes called "swamp coolers", evaporative coolers are an ideal choice for some greenhouse gardeners. The evaporative cooler works by soaking water over a natural fiber pad and blowing air through it. As a consequence, it is not very effective in humid climates. In dry climates, the air blown through is quite cool and may be ideal for an attached greenhouse that is open to a home's living area.

In the Greenhouse

Living in the desert southwest, cooling during the summer months is a big issue for my greenhouse. In triple digit temperatures, I am able to maintain a ninety degree high temperature in the greenhouse by using a shade cloth, ventilation fan and a mist system. I keep the fan's thermostat set to ninety degrees and that is ideal for my set up and cooling requirements. The door of my greenhouse is a storm door on the east side of the building and I open the screened window to allow more air intake. One of the misters is in front of the door to quickly cool the air being pulled into the greenhouse. Although ninety degrees is high for some plants, it is sufficient for the warm weather vegetables and landscape plants I grow.

Evaluate your greenhouse cooling requirements, your budget and your resources. With a bit of ingenuity, you can enjoy your greenhouse all summer long.

Warming Cold Conditions

The colder your climate, the more of a challenge you face with keeping your greenhouse warm. The introduction of heaters can be expensive, so it is a good idea to implement other methods first to reduce the amount of heat needed by a heater. Only heat the space to the minimum temperature the plants require to save money and resources.

Preventing Heat Loss

The number one way to reduce heating costs is to conserve heat. Seal up any cracks that allow heat to escape and cold to infiltrate. For wood, use caulk to fill cracks and at the edge of glass or polycarbonate, use silicon. Not sure where the infiltration is occurring? Carry incense around the greenhouse, holding it at each seam, crack, nook and cranny. You will then be able to visually see the air move as the smoke from the incense moves with the draft. Those are the spots you need to seal! Once you have sealed up all the suspected culprits, check again for any air infiltration.

Do not enter the greenhouse at night during cold spells. Air temperature drops significantly at night. By opening the door at night, you will be letting all the "hard-earned" warm air out and letting in a blast of cold air. This can also be a shock for plants. Remember that plants in the greenhouse have it easy in their cushy, temperature regulated space!

Glazing (window surface) is another location of heat loss. Greenhouse supply stores sell bubble insulator that resembles shipping bubble wrap. Placing this insulator on the glazing provides an additional insulating layer that still allows light through. If your north wall is also a glazing wall, foil backed or foam insulators can be used. Foil backed products will also reflect light back into the greenhouse. Another option is to temporarily put up a sheet of polyethylene on the inside of the greenhouse frame creating an insulating air barrier between the glazing and the inside of the greenhouse. The type of glazing also dictates how easily heat is transferred out of the greenhouse. Single-paned glass will transfer more heat than triple-wall polycarbonate. I have also seen cold climate greenhouse gardeners cover their structures with the pool covers that look like heavy-duty bubble wrap.

You may also consider a thermometer in the greenhouse with a remote alarm. Locate the remote alarm inside the main house to notify you if the temperature drops below the specified minimum temperature. The sooner you are able to react to damaging temperatures, the better.

Thermal Mass

The new energy efficient spec homes with passive solar heating are a great place to borrow ideas for the greenhouse. A basic example of thermal mass is a couple of black barrels filled with water. During the day, the sun heats the water inside the barrels and at night, the water releases the heat back into the air. Make sure the thermal mass does not touch an outside wall, as it will quickly transfer the heat away.

Even though barrels take up valuable floor space, keep in mind that it is an efficient and cost-effective method of regulating the temperature of the greenhouse. Your container can be just about anything that holds water and can be sealed. Metal drums, plastic barrels and even sealed trashcans containing water are potential thermal mass. A bench can also be placed on top to offer additional plant space.

In a solar greenhouse concept, the north wall is an insulated wall to help prevent the transfer of heat away through the glazing. Oftentimes the north wall will be made of bricks. The bricks act as thermal mass, collecting heat during the day.

Even though I mentioned it before, I say it again. I recommend that your first winter with the greenhouse you experiment with what you need to keep your greenhouse at an ideal temperature before investing in any expensive plants that are sensitive to cold temperatures. My first winter before I added any thermal mass, I experienced a sudden drop in temperature that caused frost damage on about half of my plants. Most pulled through, however I did lose some of them.

In my own greenhouse, I use a large trashcan, some five gallon buckets and several milk jugs placed under the benches. Larger containers gather and release heat slowly while smaller ones gather and release heat quickly. My goal is to keep the greenhouse ten degrees above freezing without using another heating source and minimize temperature swings at night. With temperatures in the twenties during the winter, the low temperature at night in my greenhouse is usually in the low fifties.

Many experts recommend anywhere from one gallon to four gallons of thermal mass per square foot of glazing.

Air Circulation

A small fan located at the peak of the ceiling pointed down can also assist in temperature regulation. Since the hot air rises, the fan will blow the warm air down, decreasing the number of cold spots in the greenhouse and more evenly distributing the warm air.

Greenhouses are usually sealed up in the wintertime with no outside air ventilation. It is important to promote good air circulation for good plant health. While plants do not need a fan pointed right at them, make sure air is moving around the greenhouse. Air circulation helps prevent mildew and disease. Without air circulation, plants can create air pockets around them devoid of carbon dioxide (essential for photosynthesis), which slows plant growth. I use a small solar powered fan for air circulation in the wintertime.

Heaters

In very cold climates, a heater may be an inevitable necessity. There are two types of heaters available, electric and gas. Make sure to factor into your budget the expense of running the heater! Using the above techniques will reduce the amount of time the heater must run to maintain your minimum temperature. It is also a good idea that the heater has a thermostatic control so the heater only runs when necessary.

Heaters can be a dangerous fire hazard. Make sure to follow all of the safety instructions for your heater!

Propane heaters tend to be more cost effective, however require venting. If you rely on an electrical heater, make sure to have a backup plan for when the power goes out. Keep in mind that water and electricity do not mix, make sure your heater is designed for the purpose of heating a greenhouse and exercise all the necessary safety precautions.

If possible, clear all obstructions from outside of the south wall. More sunlight will provide more natural heat. In regions where it snows, the snow on the ground will reflect more sunlight into the greenhouse. Experiment with what combination of heating methods will help you achieve the temperature required for your greenhouse. By conserving heat, you will inevitably spend less money on heating the greenhouse.

Green Thumb: Keep a backup heating source on hand during cold winter spells.

Accessories

There are oodles of accessories for the greenhouse. Some are extremely useful, others are just fun to have and add a degree of convenience to working in the greenhouse. When just starting out, it often best to select a few accessories as the essentials and then add on others as the budget allows.

Lighting

Lighting may be a luxury for some and a necessity for others. A weatherproof light fixture makes going into the greenhouse at night easier. Imagine trying to water, pot plants and examine leaves all while holding a flashlight! Some plants are light sensitive and require a certain amount of darkness in order to flower, so know your plants before turning on the light.

Some indoor gardeners will consider grow lights either for use in the greenhouse or a basement. Most greenhouses do not need grow lights, but if you live in a region where hours of daylight during winter are very limited, a grow light may be necessary to propagate plants. Mixing water and electricity is a dangerous combination so exercise caution. Grow lights need to be a few inches away from the seedlings. For this reason, you must check the plant growth daily and adjust the height of the light accordingly. When the light is too far away from the seedlings, they will elongate and "reach" for the light creating weaker stems. When the light is too close, the tips of plant leaves will burn and turn brown.

Strawberry Plant Emerging

Keeping Pests out with Screens and Insect Cloth

Screened Air Intake

As the saying goes, "An ounce of prevention is worth a pound of cure." Adding screens or insect cloth over vents and window openings will aid greatly in keeping pests out of your greenhouse.

Circulation Fans

Air circulation promotes good plant health. With stagnant air, there are actually air pockets around the plant leaves devoid of carbon dioxide. Carbon dioxide is essential to the photosynthesis process, which is how a plant converts light into energy necessary for plant growth. Air circulation helps to discourage mildew growth. A healthy plant is also more resistant to disease and pests.

Check the underside of plant leaves for pest problems.

Looking up Close with Magnifiers

A small magnifying glass has its place in the greenhouse, if only to examine the underside of leaves for pest problems. Many greenhouse pests are very tiny!

It is also fun to take an up close look at what is growing inside the greenhouse.

Instrumentation

Thermometers and hygrometers are fantastic tools to assist in evaluating the conditions inside the greenhouse. Thermometers measure temperature and hygrometers measure humidity. Many greenhouse thermometers include a built in hygrometer.

Instrumentation will aid in deciding greenhouse temperature and plant placement.

If you only get one greenhouse accessory, it should definitely be a minimum/maximum thermometer. In addition to providing the current temperature, a minimum/maximum also records the low temperature and the high temperature. With the minimum/maximum function, you will not need to go into the greenhouse during the middle of the day or night to read the temperature. Newer, high-end thermometers have remote units that can broadcast readings up to three hundred feet away.

Also available are probes and meters that can be inserted into the soil to measure moisture and pH. Many gardeners prefer to measure soil moisture simply by inserting a finger into the soil; other gardeners prefer a soil probe. If you choose to use a soil probe, be aware that not all plants needs the same amount of moisture.

Light meters are used to measure light levels in different areas of the greenhouse. If you have plants that prefer more light than others, the light meter will assist in finding the proper location for them within the greenhouse. A light meter is also useful when a shade cloth is in place on the greenhouse and will assist in evaluating how much light the shade cloth reduces and if that is an acceptable level. As an aside, polycarbonate diffuses sunlight, filling more of the shady areas in the greenhouse with light and reduces the intensity of direct sunlight.

Gardening Tools

Any gardener knows there are a gazillion gardening tools on the market! Here is what I recommend that you keep in the greenhouse to get you started:

• Hand Trowel – Get one with a comfortable handle for working the soil and scooping potting mix.

• Water Wand – Choose one with variable settings including a gentle shower and a fine mist.

• Hose – It is tempting to get a cheap garden hose. I suggest spending a couple extra dollars to get a sturdy hose otherwise you may have to replace it sooner than you think.

• Garden Scissors – A set of sharp scissors are great for pruning leaves, cutting flowers and harvesting vegetables.

• Pruning Shears – Choose a set of shears with sharp blades and comfortable handles. It is important to maintain sharp blades so the shears cut instead of crush branches.

Hand Trowel

Timers

Timers have a multitude of automation uses. For those requiring automated watering or misting, a timer that attaches to the host spigot regulates the flow of water during specified times throughout the day. Electronic timers are useful for heaters, fans and other electronic devices. Most timers run on batteries, so check them regularly.

Propagation Tools

When starting seeds out of season, a heating mat is quite useful. They are waterproof and placed underneath the seed tray to warm the soil. Although similar to a heating pad, do not attempt to use a heating pad because they are not waterproof! Thermostatic controls are also available for heating mats for more precise heating. The heating mat needs to be designed specifically for this application.

Open topped boxes made from cedar are excellent for holding seed starting mix and are able to take the constant moisture required by seedlings. Peat pellets and flats with individual cells are also great for starting seeds.

Propagation chambers range from inexpensive seed trays covered with clear plastic lids to pricey cabinets that regulate temperature and humidity.

Potting Benches

Although a potting bench is not a necessity, it is mighty convenient! Instead of needing to

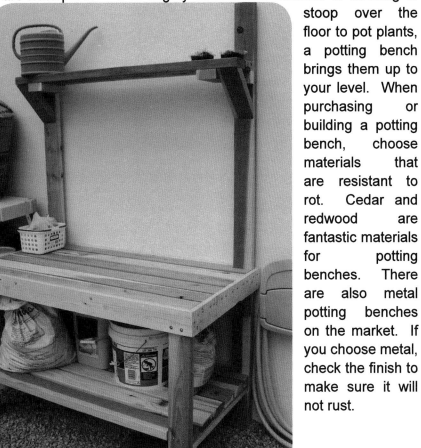

Redwood Potting Bench

stoop over the floor to pot plants, a potting bench brings them up to your level. When purchasing or building a potting bench, choose materials that are resistant to rot. Cedar and redwood are fantastic materials for potting benches. There are also metal potting benches on the market. If you choose metal, check the finish to make sure it will not rust.

A Touch of Whimsy

Sometimes you just have to have a little something cute or humorous. Consider tucking a little statue or pot ornament in among the plants or pick out a special container to use in your greenhouse.

Special Considerations When Growing Under Glass

Growing plants under glass is a whole different animal than growing outdoors. While certain aspects are much easier, such as the absence of large pests, lack of frost and more consistent temperatures, greenhouses have their own environmental and planning challenges.

Deciding the Rules of the Greenhouse

Because of the high humidity and close quarters of the greenhouse, pests and diseases can quickly spiral out of control. With a few simple ground rules, you can help prevent a lot of problems by not letting them start at all.

When friends and family find out you have a greenhouse, they will be tempted to give gifts of plants. Encourage them to instead give seeds, pots, tools and supplies.

Think long and hard before taking an outside plant into a greenhouse (unless the sole use of the greenhouse is to overwinter plants.) If you really must have the plant in the greenhouse, inspect it thoroughly for any signs of pests and diseases, checking the undersides of the leaves. Also wash the plant off. If you have planting beds in the greenhouse, consider keeping the plant in a container, as it can be difficult to discover soil-borne diseases until it is too late.

Discourage people from giving you their sick plants to put in your greenhouse. If the plant has a disease, it could quickly spread to the other plants. Unhealthy plants can rapidly develop pest problems since they are less resistant to attack, which translates to more pests in your greenhouse space.

If you or your greenhouse visitors use tobacco products, make sure to give hands a good washing. Many plants, including tomatoes and peppers, are relatives of the tobacco plant and it is possible to transfer the tobacco mosaic virus to them.

Layout

Although it may seem obvious, the layout of the greenhouse is very important. It dictates where plants live, supplies are stored and potting takes place. Typically, the south wall is dedicated solely for plantings since it is the most light-filled area of the greenhouse. Since the north wall receives less light, it usually gets dedicated to a potting bench, plants that require less light and seed propagation. The north wall is also a good place for a trellis for climbing plants.

Beds vs. Benches

Both planting beds and benches with containers have their advantages and disadvantages.

Planting beds provide a more permanent home for plants and does away with the need to continuously pot up plants. Moisture is held in the soil more readily and temperatures are steadier around the roots than with containers.

One pitfall of planting beds is crop rotation. Plants cannot be placed in the same location year after year without amending the soil and working in compost. Without rotating food crops, nutrients deplete and soil borne diseases can take over. Also, invasive plants could potentially take over the greenhouse planting beds. Plants may require more room since there is more space for roots to spread out, however this is also a plus since plants can grow in an unrestricted environment.

When using benches, there is storage space underneath and a sun-sheltered space for shade-loving plants. Containers offer a lot of flexibility in moving plants around. Should you find a plant does not like the sun and heat, it can quickly be moved to another area of the greenhouse. There is less bending and stooping with the plants elevated.

With containers, the soil is contained meaning soil-borne diseases do not easily transfer to other plants. Containers do dry out more quickly than planting beds, so moisture levels need to be monitored closely during hot weather.

Another option is raised beds. While not for everyone, constructing elevated beds gives those who prefer a planting bed the ability to access the plants without bending over. Raised beds instead of in-ground beds provide gardeners requiring wheelchair accessibility easier access to the planting area.

Benches with
Storage Below

Layout with Benches along South
Wall and Short Peninsulas

I personally prefer containers with benches as I always seem to change my mind about what is going on inside and I grow a lot of things that will not stay in the greenhouse permanently. Many people prefer planting beds because it better mimics a natural growing environment and some plants are just not suited to growing in containers. Containers can also "dwarf" the growth of a plant since there is less room for root growth. While this is an advantage for large plants that you would like to keep small, it can be a disadvantage for some food crops.

Configuration Ideas

How you configure your beds or benches is a matter of personal preference and the size of the greenhouse. Placing benches around the edge works for small greenhouses, however with larger greenhouses, this will leave the center as wasted space. An island of benches in the middle will provide more usable space in a large greenhouse.

In long narrow greenhouses, a peninsula layout may work better. Having a long bench along the south wall with benches jutting out perpendicularly will provide more bench space but still allow access to the plants in the back.

Hanging Baskets

Containers can even be placed on the floor. If you have tall plants that need all the "head room" they can get, an area dedicated for this is ideal.

Don't forget to look up! Consider suspending a bar for hanging plants, every square inch of the greenhouse is valuable. Continually examine how you are using the space to determine if there is a better way to configure your greenhouse.

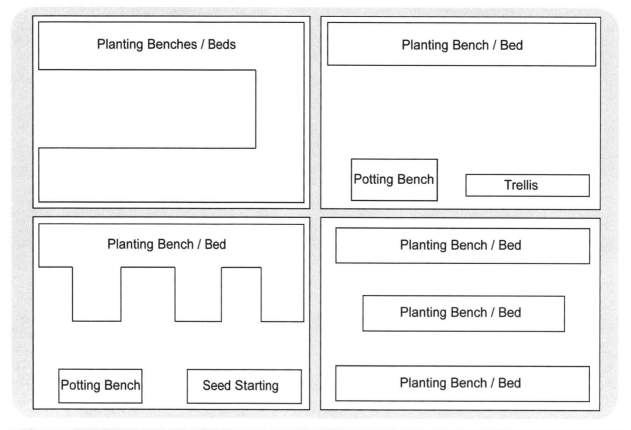

Watering & Humidity

One of the biggest challenges for new gardeners is watering. Most plants do not need water every day. Make a habit of checking the plants' soil before watering. Either push your finger into the soil up to the first knuckle to check the moisture level or use a moisture probe. Over watering can be just as detrimental as under watering!

Repeat after me, "I will not over water my plants…"

Generally speaking, plants love humidity! Humidity also greatly affects how often you need to water. Soil does not dry out as quickly in higher humidity so plants do not need to be watered as often.

Invest in a nice watering wand. The long arm makes reaching plants in the back of a bench or bed much easier. When watering plants, a gentle spray like a rainfall keeps from disturbing the soil surface. Switch to a delicate mist when watering seedlings since they are so fragile. Water at the base of plants instead of overhead to keep the leaves from getting soaked as this can encourage fungal diseases.

Green Thumb:

When the temperature is warm, humidity aids in cooling the air. For a quick burst in humidity, spray the floor down with water. With cooler air, less humidity is ideal so the air stays warm.

Microclimates

Just as is sounds, microclimates are little climates within a larger space. The north side of the greenhouse receives less light than the south side. Underneath a bench will be very shady and cool, while hanging plants will experience more heat. Be aware of the temperature and light nuances in the greenhouse and then use them to your advantage! Tuck shade-lovers like ginger into those spots that other plants detest and leave the warm, sunny spots for tomatoes and others that adore all that sunshine.

Microclimates can also change by the season and as plants grow. The very act of watering can raise humidity and lower temperature. Larger plants create more shade. Be proactive in observing light, shadows and temperature variations, and then arrange your plants in the space where they will be happy and thrive.

These lettuce seedlings are happily growing
in the cool shade of the benches.

Seasonal Considerations and Hardiness Zones

As the seasons change, so does the environment in the greenhouse. The changes are not as drastic as outside when growing under glass, however there are considerations that must be taken into account.

Most of us will have wintertime temperatures in the greenhouse hovering in the fifties as well as reduced hours of daylight. For heat-loving plants like tomatoes, this means much slower growth and reduced production. You may still end up with the ultimate prize of a vine-ripe tomato in the winter! Instead of fighting with the temperatures, embrace them. Take the opportunity to grow plants that love cooler weather like lettuce and chrysanthemums.

The USDA has divided the United States into a series of hardiness zones based on the average lowest temperature for the region with the lowest zone numbers being the coldest. (In the resources section, I have provided a link to the USDA's website in order to determine your hardiness zone.) While hardiness zones are more pertinent to outside gardening, they do play a part in indoor gardening as well.

A hardiness zone of four experiences minimum temperatures in the range of −30 to −20 degrees Fahrenheit where as a hardiness zone of eight only has minimum temperature of 10 to 20 degrees. A Zone 8 greenhouse will require a lot less to keep it warm than a Zone 4 greenhouse.

If this is the first winter with your greenhouse, grow plants that are hardy to cold conditions until you have experienced how your climate affects the temperature inside your greenhouse. Armed with this experience, you are then better able to judge if cold tender plants will do well in your space.

If you have a freestanding greenhouse, there is more expense to keep it warm in the wintertime. As I previously discussed, heat your greenhouse only to the minimum your plants will tolerate. If you live in Zone 4, keeping a Zone 10 plant in your greenhouse will be much more difficult as these plants are extremely sensitive to the cold.

Conversely, I live in Zone 7b, and to keep plants that are more suited to colder regions in the northern United States, I will be fighting a loosing battle because I would not be able to keep the temperature low enough for those plants in the summertime. Also, a lot of plants from northern regions require a "chilling" period or dormancy period that my zone would not be able to provide.

Growing Guidelines

Now that the greenhouse space is in order and ready to use, it is time to grow something! While an empty greenhouse may be intimidating, we all have to start somewhere. And don't worry if a plant does not work out, it will make a nice addition to the compost pile and become great fertilizer for future plants.

This section will assist you in getting started with the greenhouse production process. From seed starting to pollination to trellising, it will guide you through each step of growing plants under glass.

Growing Concepts

From starting seeds to harvesting your bounty, all your outdoor gardening knowledge will come in handy. And if you do not have a lot of gardening experience, that's okay too. I will cover all the bases on getting those beautiful plants growing in your indoor space.

Keeping Tabs with a Garden Journal

Journaling will come quite easy for some folks. For others, writing just does not come naturally. If you fall into the latter category, not to worry! At the minimum, keep a chart for each plant you grow in the greenhouse, when the seeds germinate, temperatures and when crops were harvested. It is often easy to say, "Oh, I will remember that." Don't neglect your garden journal! With the information you collect about how plants perform in your space, you can quickly reference your journal in future seasons to know what plants were successful for you.

Once a month, make a note of the conditions in the greenhouse. Record the temperature inside as well as outside, and any climate modifications (i.e. heating, ventilation, etc.) This will assist you in deciding when to start what plants and notice the warming and cooling trends in the greenhouse.

Typically I carry a small notebook into the greenhouse with me to jot down a couple quick notes about any new developments. This includes when seeds germinate, when I harvest something or when a new flower opens.

Take your journal to the greenhouse and write down notes regarding your activities with plants. For example, my prized mesquite trees did not start out as such! I had a very difficult time getting those seeds to germinate. Over the course of three months, I documented what I did for each attempt: scarification methods, date of sowing, the material seeds were sowed in, temperature and germination dates. Each time I tried something different, I looked back at my past attempts to evaluate what went wrong and what went right. Now I have a system and am able to get the mesquite seeds to readily germinate.

As I document my plants, I note the common name, botanical name and where the seeds were obtained. That way if I choose to grow the plant again, there is no question as to which variety I liked so much. Sometimes I even staple empty seed packets to the pages!

You can also use your garden journal to plan future growing endeavors. Say you see a variety of plant you would love to grow, write it down. It can be very overwhelming going through seed catalogs. Perhaps even cut out the photos that inspire you so when the time comes to order seeds, you recall just why you loved that plant.

My point is this: whether you love to write, prefer charts or even scrapbooking, do what works for you. No one is going to judge how you keep your information. It is just important that you keep information! At the back of this book are some examples to help you get your journal started.

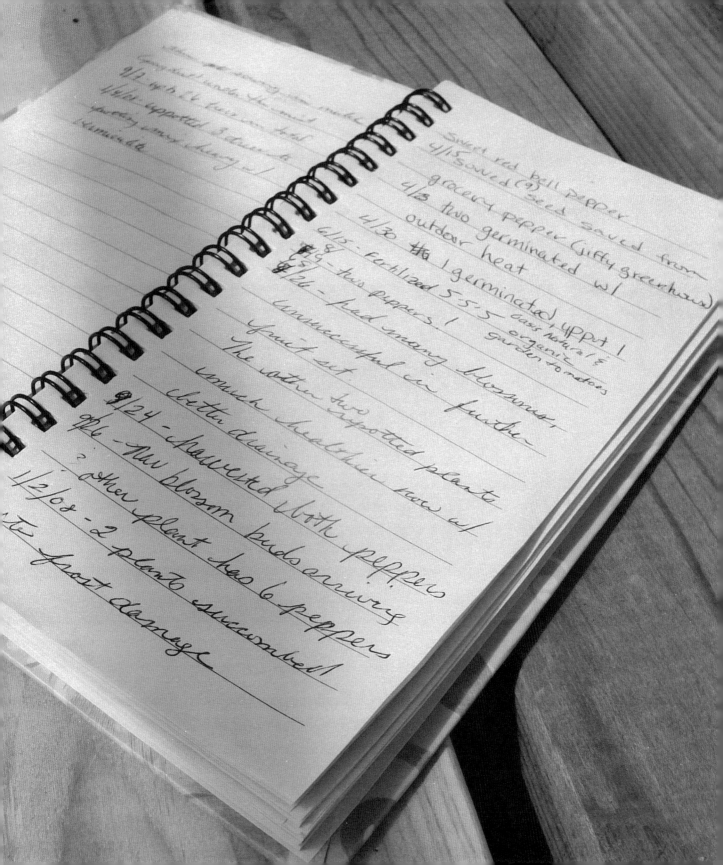

What is in a Name? Botanical Name, That is.

The botanical name refers to the scientific name of a plant. Most of us know names of plants by their common names. For example, we all know tomatoes as just that, tomatoes. The tomato's botanical name is Solanum lycopersicum.

By seeing the botanical name, you will begin to recognize that similar plants are in the same genus. Relatives of tomatoes are potatoes (Solanum tuberosum) and eggplants (Solanum melongena), each in the Solanum genus. A particular variety's botanical name such as a cherry tomato is depicted as Solanum lycopersicum var. cerasiforme, with the variety's name, or cultivar, after "var." term.

A lot can be recognized by the botanical name. A potato is a tuber, and its botanical name is Solanum tuberosum, tuberosum referring to a tuber. The second word in the botanical name is the specific epithet, which identifies the species and is quite often very descriptive of the plants' characteristics.

Examples of Descriptive Specific Epithets

Botanical Epithet	Descriptive Meaning
azurea	blue
decidua	deciduous
fragrans	fragrant
mexicana	from Mexico
perennis	perennial
vulgaris	common

If you are interested in learning more about descriptive species epithets, information can be located in the References section of this book.

Tomatoes are related to a lot of other plants. Common tomato diseases can be transmitted to peppers and eggplants. It is a good rule of green thumb to know your plants' relatives.

Decoding the Seed Packet

The back of the seed packet is your first source of information regarding growing the seeds inside. Become familiar with the terms commonly used on packets and you will become a seed starting pro in no time at all.

At the top of the packet is the name, variety and sometimes the botanical name followed by a brief description of the mature plant. Below the description will be a chart providing you with information vital to the plant's health.

Light	Sun	Depth	Germination	Height
Full Sun	12"	1/4"	7-10 Days	12-18"

Light: Will either be Full Sun (6 hours+ of sunlight), Part Sun (4-6 hours), Part Shade (2-4 hours) or Full Shade (less than two hours). This is important because in the wrong light conditions, the plant will not grow to its optimum form, or worse, not grow at all.

Spacing: When plants are young, the spacing may not seem correct. The number provided is for mature plants. Pay particular attention to spacing as crowded plants fight for soil nutrients and air circulation around the foliage decreases creating ideal conditions for fungus and mildew. You may also see a notation for row spacing, which is typical for food crops making it easier to walk between the plants without compacting the soil at the base of the plants. When growing in containers, row spacing is not applicable.

Depth: The depth refers to how deep to sow the seeds. Do not sow deeper than the recommended depth as the seedling may not have enough energy to get past the extra soil.

Germination: How many days does it take to make a plant grow? The seed packet will tell you! Some plants do not follow the rules, some seeds take longer and others shorter. I have had seeds germinate in three days that are supposed to take over a week!

Height: Just how big is the plant going to get? The seed packet will give you a size range, and the reason is because conditions that the plant is grown in will affect its mature height. Containers, pruning, light, water and overall health affect just how tall a plant will grow.

Below the information chart will be gardening notes with further information about starting the seeds. This will often include when to sow, when to harvest (for food crops), what temperature range the soil must fall into in order for seeds to germinate and other helpful hints. Stamped on the flap is the "packaged for" year.

Sometimes the seed packet can be lacking. I have purchased seeds before with very limited information thinking they were to be sowed in the spring. Come to find out (after lack of germination) that they were fall germinating during cool temperatures. If you have any doubt in your mind about what to do with seeds or when to sow them, search online or check a plant reference book to answer your questions.

Starting Seeds

I just love baby plants! For me, it is so rewarding growing from seed and not to mention cheaper than buying plants.

A perfect example of this is the mesquite trees I am growing for my landscape. Most of the trees I am growing came from seed pods dropped from other mesquites. A local nursery charges nearly fifty dollars for a six foot tree with a truck barely an inch in diameter. My husband and I estimated that we needed around thirty trees for our landscape, so you can easily see how growing from seed can be more cost effective.

Using a good seed-starting medium, fill a tray or flat and moisten. Sow the seeds according to the depth indicated on the seed packet and let nature take over.

Should your seed packet lack the information of the sowing depth, the general rule is the width of the seed is how deep the seed is sowed. Mist the tray twice a day, being careful not to disturb the soil. If you prefer, cover the tray with a clear plastic lid or plastic wrap. Seedlings are just a few days away!

Many companies offer a wide variety of seed starting products. There are peat pellets that expand in water and plastic domes that hold in humidity. Try out a few different products and see what works best for you.

Personally, I use a finely ground mulch in a tray for starting seeds. Once the seedlings are large enough to handle, I transplant them into a soil mix.

Some seedlings do not respond well to transplanting, such as root vegetables like carrots and radishes. Others like lettuces are just too small to handle. In these cases, direct sowing provides better success. Sow the seeds where they will be grown to maturity and keep moist during the germination period. A seed packet will likely indicate if it needs to be direct sown.

Germinating seeds and seedlings do not like to dry out. Use a gentle mist to keep the soil moist without disturbing the delicate seedlings. Although I cannot personally attest to a difference, some gardeners report that "petting" seedlings encourages stronger growth. All the more reason to love your plants!

Scarification & Stratification

Seeds Soaking in Water

Seeds are dormant and we have to break that dormancy in order to get the seed to germinate. A seed will start growing when conditions are right for survival. For most seeds, moisture and warmth are enough to get it going, however other seeds need a bit more help from us to get them started.

Seed stratification is when you simulate that a seed has been through the cold winter months and have fooled it into thinking that it is now spring. You are essentially telling it, "Time to grow!" Moisten a bit of seed starting medium and put it in a plastic bag with the seeds and stick it in the refrigerator, usually three weeks does the trick. The seed packet will typically let you know how long the chilling period needs to be. After the chilling period, transfer them to the tray or pot that you are using to grow them and place in a warm location. Some seeds require heat stratification, which involves placing the seeds in a very warm location instead of cold.

Scarification is done on seeds that have a very thick outer coating that water does not easily penetrate. File or sand an edge of the seed coating until you see the lighter layer underneath. Proceed by soaking the seeds overnight and when the seeds have swelled to twice their size, they are ready to sow. Another type of scarification is a boiling water treatment, which can be done by heating a cup of water and dropping the seeds in. This also achieves breaking the outer coating of the seed to allow moisture in.

For seeds like my mesquite trees that are difficult to germinate, I have soaked seeds in a cup of water set in a warm spot for a couple days until I begin to see growth, and then I sow them. This gives them a better shot at growing up.

Seed Viability

The viability of the seeds is how readily they will germinate. The fresher the seed, the more viable it will be. Some seed catalogs will report the germination rate in terms of percentage, i.e. 85% germination rate. Viability can also be affected by the seeds source. Many hybrid plants produce sterile seed.

You can also test the viability of your seeds by placing several in between damp paper towels in a plastic bag. Put the bag in a warm spot for a few days and then check to see how many seeds began to germinate. If over half start to grow, you're good to go!

Damping Off

When seedlings begin to grow, it is important to give them good circulation. Stagnant, moist air may cause damping off. Damping off is caused by a fungus and wet conditions. It affects the base of the seedlings, making the seedling fall over and die.

Green Thumb:

If you use a tray with a lid to germinate seeds, either prop open the lid or completely remove it once seedlings emerge.

Cuttings

Some plants are just really, really difficult to grow from seed, so cuttings are the way to go to propagate some plants.

Examine the plant from which you will be taking the cutting. Make sure it is healthy otherwise you will just be creating a clone of the problems. Look for a branch or stem with several good, sturdy leaves and remove any flowers. (You want the new plant to use energy to create roots for the first couple months of its new life.) Make a diagonal cut just above a leaf node. Remove two sets of leaves from the bottom end of the cutting. Now place in a glass of water, changing out the water every couple days to prevent mold and rot. Once several roots have grown, transplant it into soil.

You can also place cuttings directly in soil by dipping the end of the cutting in powdered rooting hormone and then put the cutting a couple inches in soil. Once the plant starts to grow again, you know you have roots. Another test is after a few weeks, gently pull on the cutting and if you feel resistance, roots have grown and taken hold in the soil.

How to Transplant

Step One: Prepare the soil that will be the seedling's new home.

Step Two: Gently lift the seedling by one of the leaves and loosen the soil around the base.

Step Three: Place the seedling in the prepared pot and gently press it into place.

Transplanting Seedlings

When a plant germinates, the first set of leaves is called the seed leaves or cotyledons. The seed leaves are what store the energy that the seed uses to germinate. They are usually round and not the same shape of the leaves that the plant will have. The next set to grow is the true leaves, and they are the true shape of the leaves of the plant.

When your seedling is large enough to handle, it is time to transplant. Depending on the size of the seedling, this can be when it has grown seed leaves, a first set of true leaves, or a second set of true leaves. Cucumber seedlings are very large and can usually be handled early on, however delphinium seedlings are delicate and need to grow a bit larger. Use your judgment and decide when you can handle the seedlings without damaging them.

If you use peat pellets to start your seeds, transplanting is easy. Pick up the pellet seedling and all to transplant it. What could be simpler?

If you have used a tray, a little more delicate measure is required. Prepare the pot you are moving the seedling to by moistening some potting mix and fill the container, leaving a hole for the seedling. When handling the seedling, hold it by one of the leaves and not the stem. At this stage of growth, the stem is very delicate. A plant can recover much easier from damage to the leaf than it can from damage to the stem. Grasp the seedling by the leaf and using a wooden skewer, lift the soil until the seedling easily pulls away. Do not yank as this will end up with your plant in pieces! Hold the seedling in the new container and fill the soil in around the tiny root. Now your plant will happily grow in its new home.

A Good Foundation with Good Soil

Potting Soil

Good gardening soil is not just dirt but is a complex living organism. Soil contains millions of microbes that break down organic matter creating a nutrient rich environment that feeds plants.

Most gardeners use topsoil in their planting beds. Make it a habit at the end of each growing season to turn in compost. This adds new nutrients and keeps your soil fertile. If your soil drains poorly, the addition of horticultural grade sand (found at garden centers) will assist water to reach the roots of plants.

If you container garden in your greenhouse and make your own potting mix, a good starting point is a half and half mix of soil and compost and a cup or two of perlite. For higher water retention, add vermiculite. If you find you need better drainage, add course sand. Cacti and succulents require a drier environment, so add more sand.

The other part of the soil equation is pH. The pH scale measures acidity and alkalinity on a scale of 0 to 14, with 7 being neutral. For example, citrus is an acid, and on the scale, orange juice is just under 4. Most plants prefer soil just under 7 (slightly acidic) on the pH scale. A lot of desert plants like alkaline soil, above 7, and plants like blueberries thrive in acidic soil, under 7.

You can test the pH of your soil with a soil meter or have your local cooperative extension run tests on a soil sample. The tests that the cooperative extension run are thorough and include all kinds of useful information including the nutrients in your soil and recommendations for amending your soil.

To change the pH of soil quickly, amendments may need to be added. To raise a soil's pH, work in garden lime. Garden sulfur, sawdust, leaf mold and peat moss will all lower soil pH. To change it over time, the addition of finished compost every six months will recondition soil and move it towards pH neutral.

Make sure that if you reuse your potting mix, not to use it for the same kind of plant. Soil from an old tomato plant should not be used to pot a new tomato plant. This helps prevent the transfer of diseases specific to that kind of plant.

As a side note, peat moss is a common garden soil amendment, however it is not a renewable resource. It is harvested from wetlands and wetlands are fragile ecosystems. Disruption of wetlands destroys wildlife habitats. Consider using an alternative made from coir (coconut husks).

Growing with Containers

Container gardening offers the flexibility of being able to move plants around and grow without gardening beds, but containers are not without their own set of challenges. Containers dry out much faster than in-ground plants, and therefore require more diligent attention to their water requirements. Attention also needs to be paid to the roots. Some plants like tight quarters, however most do not like to be pot bound. If you lift the plant from its pot and the roots are a tangled, nasty mass at the bottom of the pot, then the plant is pot bound and it is definitely time to pot up.

The biggest issue with containers is drainage. Without adequate drainage, a plant can become waterlogged and suffer. Soil can also become rancid. When you water your plants, you should see water come out of the drainage holes. If you don't, it is time to address the problem!

I had a couple tomato plants that suddenly turned yellow and sickly. I tried everything I could think of and nothing seemed to help them. I eventually set the pots on the ground and gave them a very thorough soaking and quickly I noticed an acrid smell. The pots I was using had built in trays that were attached to the bottom and the trays were clogging the drainage holes.

I ripped off the trays and lifted the plant from the pots and whew was it stinky! If I had caught the problem sooner, I may have been able to save the plants, but they ended up in the compost bin with a lesson learned.

Some people swear by adding gravel to the bottom of a pot for better drainage. My opinion is that it just makes the pot heavy and takes away from space for root growth. Fillers do have their place for large pots. If your plants have a shallow root system, there is no sense in filling the entire pot with mix. In all truth, a good loose mix with perlite should provide ample drainage. Regular garden soil compacts far too easily for containers. Either purchase potting mix or create your own. You can prevent soil from falling out through the drainage holes with either a pottery shard or a piece of screen.

Just about anything that holds soil can be used as a container, it just needs drainage holes. If it lacks holes, drill them into the bottom. The most common off the shelf containers are either plastic or terracotta. Terracotta has more visual appeal, but dries out very quickly and can break. Plastic is durable, lightweight and retains moisture but may lack aesthetic appeal. Many manufacturers are now making pots out of plastic or resin that look remarkably like terracotta.

As a plant grows and matures, it is likely to outgrow its container. If the roots are coming out the drainage holes, it is definitely overdue to pot up! Choose a larger container, add soil to the bottom and lift the plant from the old pot. If the roots are tightly wound, tease the roots out a bit with your fingers and place the plant into the new pot. Add soil around the edges, pressing gently to remove any air pockets and then water well. Make sure the soil level at the base of the plant is the same in its new pot. If soil is too high on the stem, it can promote rot.

When a plant lives in a pot for over a year, the soil condition may decline and require repotting. If your plant tolerates its roots being disturbed, lift the plant from its container and prune out any dead or coiling roots. Prune no more than 25% of its root system. Prepare fresh potting mix and fertilizer in the pot, and then repot the plant in its container.

Successive Sowing

For vegetable crops that harvest at the same time, a gardening technique called successive sowing is ideal for extending the number of weeks that a crop can be harvested. Ideal crops for successive sowing are root crops and leaf crops. Radishes, carrots and other root crops mature at the same time. By sowing smaller numbers every couple of weeks, you will have smaller numbers of carrots to harvest over a longer period of time. Lettuce and other greens also work well with successive sowing to spread out the harvest.

Growing Vertical

When selecting plants to grow, it is important to know your type. Plants are classified as determinate or indeterminate. Determinate plants only grow to a specific height. Indeterminate plants are vines that will continually grow in length until pruned. In a greenhouse, indeterminate plants can sprawl and quickly overrun a space. Some varieties of plants, like tomatoes, are available as both determinate and indeterminate. Look at determinate varieties classified as "bush" or "dwarf". Roma tomatoes grow to 4 feet tall, but stay in a bushy form. However if you love a particular plant that grows in an indeterminate vine form, don't despair – grow vertical!

Trellising and Training

A trellis frees up space by growing vines vertically. Vertical growth promotes good air circulation for better plant health.

One method of growing vertical is training your vines up a trellis. Place your trellis where it will not shade the greenhouse space, such as on the north wall or in the center of the greenhouse in a north-south orientation. Make sure your trellis is secure and sturdy because it will get heavy with vines growing all over it. A trellis can either be bought pre-made or constructed from wood, sturdy wire, plastic or composite. If you opt for a pre-made trellis, make sure it is large enough to accommodate the vines as they grow. Most garden center trellises are on the smallish side.

Grow your vines in either a planting bed beneath the trellis or place the container in front of the trellis. Some vines will look for something to climb and attach, twist and grow around what ever it finds. Other vines will need to be trained and tied to the trellis. Use soft ties, plastic tree tape or cushioned wire to tie your vines so as to not damage the stems. If you like to reuse materials, old nylons work great!

Trellising is a great option for growing small melons such as honeydews and cantaloupes. Just make sure to support the melons as they grow as the weight can pull them right off the stem. A sling made from old nylons works great because as the melon grows, the sling expands.

To provide a trellis for a smaller plant like peas, a tall tripod made from bamboo stakes provides plenty of support and gives the vines a place to grow. Form a tripod with three stakes and tie together two to three inches from the top, then place over the plant.

Staking, Cages & Strings

Sometimes even bushy plants need a little extra support. Stakes can be any variety of materials, bamboo being one of the more cost effective depending upon the source. Push the stake into the soil two inches away from the stem of the plant. Use soft ties such as twine or padded wire, not bare wire as it will damage the stems. In a figure eight pattern with one loop around the stake and the other around the stem, loosely tie the plant to the stake. You could even grow a container of bamboo to make your own stakes. Just harvest the bamboo and allow it to dry out before using.

One of the more popular plant support methods is a tomato cage. These are just as they sound, a round cage made of wire. I have yet to experience luck with these with tomatoes because the plants get too heavy and the weight deforms the cage. Containers with cages can also become top heavy. They are great for lighter weight plants that just need a bit of support keeping the stems upright. Flowers like tall carnations can get top heavy when in bloom and cages can keep them supported and beautiful.

Long vines can be trained up a string or sturdy twine. Keep the plant pruned to one main vine. Tie a string to a hook or rafter in the ceiling of the greenhouse and stake the other end in the soil next to the plant you want to train, leaving a fair amount of slack in the string. As the vine grows, gently wrap it around the string, which will begin to take up the slack. When the vine reaches the top of the string, pinch out the end of the vine so it will not grow any longer. This is a real space saver! Imagine a cucumber vine growing up instead of all over the floor of your greenhouse.

Upside-down Pots

One of the newer crazes in gardening is upside-down pots. These are soft-sided pots with a hole in the bottom and a hook in the top to hang from a rafter or overhang. The plant goes in the bottom upside-down and soil goes in the pot. It seems like a very unnatural way for a plant to grow, but I knew I had to try them out. I purchased three to test with indeterminate tomato plants. I found that the plants need to be around a foot tall before they get transplanted into the upside pots and it seems they get too much shade otherwise. My tomatoes produced very well and the height that the plant hangs at made it easy for me to tend to the plant. I did need to use a watering wand though to reach the top of the pot to water the plants and the soft sides can degrade over time.

Upside-down Planter

Male or Female?

Identifying male and female flowers is very important for the pollination process. Once you know what to look for, spotting which flower is which will become second nature.

This female blossom on a watermelon vine is easy to identify with the tiny, immature fruit behind the flower.

The male blossoms on this watermelon vine do not have immature fruits and the center of the flower is covered in yellow powdery pollen.

Pollination

Out in the open, pollination is taken care of by bees, wind and other insects. When gardening inside, you have to take over the pollination duties.

In order to pollinate flowers, we have to understand a bit of flower anatomy. Flowers have male and female parts. The male part, the stamen, contains the pollen and the female part, the pistil, receives the pollen. The stamen usually looks like a long stalk inside the flower with the tip covered in powdery pollen. The pistil typically looks like a sticky disk in the center of the flower.

Some plants have flowers that contain both male and female parts. Pollination can be achieved by just tapping the stem of the flower and the pollen will transfer from the stamen to the pistil. Sweet peppers are very easy to pollinate in this manner. Another technique is to use a soft bristled artist brush in the flower to spread the pollen.

Tomatoes, although they contain both parts in the flower, are enclosed making pollination a bit more difficult. It seems that for best success, the "buzzing" of a bee's wings needs to be simulated. I purchased a small, inexpensive vibrating toothbrush from a discount store and use it by holding it against the flower to make it vibrate. The toothbrush has worked quite well and my plants are covered in tomatoes without the aid of insects.

Other plants have male flowers and female flowers requiring a bit more intervention in order to pollinate them. Look at the flowers on your plant and find a male flower with a good amount of pollen. Use a paintbrush and gently transfer the pollen onto the tip of the brush. Then find a female flower and carefully brush the pollen onto the pistil. Usually the pollen from one male flower will be enough to pollinate around three female flowers. If successful, you will begin to see fruit growth within a couple days. With melons, the female flowers are easy to identify because they have an immature fruit behind the flower. Another method of pollination is to pluck the male flower, remove its petals, and then brush it against the female flower.

A select few plants require no pollination at all! These are special cultivars created to produce fruit without the act of pollination and are very well suited to the indoor gardening environment. The variety of cucumbers (Sweet Success) growing in my greenhouse produces seedless cucumbers when no pollination occurs. When looking through seed catalogs, look for seeds ideal for greenhouse production. It will be noted in the description if pollination is not required.

Clean your pollination tools before moving to another plant. Once, I accidentally cross-pollinated Roma tomatoes and grape tomatoes. Those were some strange looking tomatoes!

This strawberry blossom contains both male and female parts. Pollination is achieved easily by rubbing a soft-bristled brush over the center of the flower to spread the pollen around.

Pruning and Pinching

The time will come when your plants will need a bit of shaping and pruning. The act of pruning encourages growth, so by pruning from the unwanted areas, you are stimulating the plant to produce growth elsewhere. You can also prevent spread of fungus by cutting off the affected foliage. Keep your tools clean. It is possible to transfer disease from one plant to another!

It is important to know how to properly prune plants. Improper pruning can damage plants. When pruning, select the branch or stem you would like to cut. Move back on the stem until you find the leaf node closest to where you would like to cut. Cut just above the node diagonally. Make sure to use sharp shears, as dull ones will tend to crush and tear stems.

Pinching is just like is sounds. To top off growth from a vine or to stimulate bushier growth on a woody plant, pinch between your thumb and forefinger just after the last leaf node on a stem. This will stop the extending growth of that stem and divert growth elsewhere to bushier growth or fruit production, depending upon the stage the plant is in. Pinching out the tips of basil plants produces a much more pleasing form and stimulates production of leaves instead of flowers, and the leaves are the tasty part for which the plant is grown.

Most gardeners prefer to allow indeterminate tomato plants to grow unmanaged, however some selective pruning can lead to better fruit production. Indeterminate tomatoes will grow suckers, stems with leaves and no flowers. In the nook, or axil, between the main stem and a

Pinching and pruning stimulates growth elsewhere on the plant.

side stem is where suckers grow. Pinch out the suckers while they are still small and the plant will use its energy for tomatoes instead of new stem and leaf growth. Pinching out the suckers also allows for better air circulation around the leaves minimizing fungus and mildew problems.

Hardening Off

When starting plants indoors for use outdoors, they must go through a hardening off period before moving outside. Plants inside have it easy and are not accustomed to hot sun, drying winds, cold nights and less frequent watering. The hardening off period consists of slowly introducing plants to the outside world after any danger of frost has passed. Check the minimum temperatures your plants will tolerate before attempting to harden them off.

Start off with introducing them to the outdoors for half a day, placing plants in a sheltered area away from strong sunlight. Follow up by a full day outside, and then move the plants back indoors. Start reducing the amount of water the plants receive, but do not allow the plants to wilt. Wilting will just add stress to the plants. Then begin allowing the plants to stay out into the evening. The final process is to allow the plants to stay outside all day and night. The process should occur over a week or two. Then they can finally be planted in the ground. Keep a close eye on the plants because containers will dry out faster outside than they will inside.

If moving plants outside and inside every day does not appeal to you, another option is use of a cold frame. Cold frames are essentially mini greenhouses that can be closed up at night to protect young, tender plants.

Tulip, Fancy Frills

Saving Seeds

If you already enjoy growing from seed, the next step is to start saving your own seeds. Did you have a plant that you really enjoyed through the growing season? Did it produce really tasty vegetables? Were the flowers really something to behold? Save the seeds and grow it again!

Issues with Hybrids

When you purchase a hybrid from a seed catalog, the seed produced by that plant might provide mixed results. The resulting plant may not be as vigorous as the parent plant, not produce as many flowers or fruit, or not grow at all. There is no reason not to experiment with seeds, just be aware that you may not get what you expect.

Catalogs also offer F1 Hybrids. F1 is the first generation of a hybrid cross and the parent plants seldom have the same characteristics and the seeds. Very commonly, the seeds produced by an F1 Hybrid will give very mixed results and will rarely have the same characteristics as the parent plant.

Drying on the Plant

To save seeds from legumes, just let the pods mature and dry right on the plant. As soon as you can hear the seeds rattle inside the pod, they're ready! Nearly all of my mesquite trees where grown from pods that I saved. Spent flower heads are the source for seeds from most flowers and herbs. Just pluck the spent flower heads and remove the seeds. Corn seeds are saved from the ears that are dried right on the stalk.

Allowing the Fruit to Mature

For most vegetables including cucumbers, melons, squash and peppers, allow the fruit to fully mature on the plant, harvest and remove the seeds. Wash the seeds and let them air dry. Some vegetables including cucumbers and green peppers are immature when they are harvested to eat, and seeds saved from them at this stage will not grow.

Seeds from fruit trees may not be worth your while to grow. Fruit trees from nurseries are typically grafted onto rootstock to produce faster growing, higher yielding fruit trees. Fruit trees are a long-term investment in time, so better to give yourself a head start with your fruit production by purchasing a tree.

Fermentation

Tomatoes require a bit more work to save the seeds, however it is worth it to continue growing a beloved variety of heirloom tomato! When the tomato is ripe, cut it open and scoop or squeeze out the seeds (gooey gelatinous stuff included) and put it in a jar with water. Stir it all up and put it out of the way because this can get pretty stinky. After a couple of days, mold will start to grow and the mix will begin to ferment. Another two or three days and the good seeds will settle to the bottom. Scoop off the goopy layer and rinse the seeds, then allow them to air dry.

The pulp that is in the tomato prevents the seeds from germinating inside the tomato. Isn't Mother Nature ingenious? However if the pulp is not cleaned off, the seeds will not germinate when you plant them, hence the need for the fermentation process.

Catching Scattered Seeds

Some flowers drop their seeds as soon as they are mature. Pansies and snapdragons, to name a few, break open quickly to scatter their seeds. To catch these seeds, tie a paper or mesh bag over the dry flower head before the seeds scatter. After a few days, cut the stem of the flower, turn the bag over and relish in your saved seed.

Storing Seeds

Seeds need to be kept in a cool, dry place. Keep your seeds in paper envelopes because plastic bags hold moisture. Label your envelopes with the name of the seed, when and where it was collected and any other tidbits of information that were useful to you when growing it.

Keep your envelopes of seeds in a paper bag or box, not plastic. The key is to keep the seeds dry. (I use a photo box for mine.) Store the box in a closet in the house as opposed to the shed or greenhouse since it gets too warm there.

Pest Management, Disease Prevention & Fertilization

Pests are inevitable. The best defense against pests and disease is prevention. Prevention involves good sanitation practices such as cleaning your tools and picking up leaf litter to stop the spread of disease from plant to plant. In the high humidity and close quarters of a greenhouse environment, it is important to employ good practices because it can be difficult to stop a problem once it has started. Water plants from the base instead of overhead as wet leaves can be a breeding ground for mold and mildew. In the quest for disease prevention, look for disease resistant varieties in the seed catalogs.

Organic vs. Synthetic

I will be the first to admit I have a serious bias to organic practices. I opt to not use pesticide to maintain a healthy balance in my greenhouse. I have heard too many stories of people using chemical pesticide to eradicate the problem only to have it come back ten-fold. The greenhouse is an ecosystem all its own and when using broad-spectrum pesticide, you not only kill pests, you kill everything that eats the pests. If you can deal with a couple insects here and there, in my opinion you will be better off in the long run. Also, just because a product is labeled organic, that does not make it non-toxic.

Sometimes, there is a pest problem that requires intervention. Should pesticide be used around food crops, make sure that it is food grade and follow the instructions as many have a specific amount of time after spraying before the food can be harvested for consumption. Consider using horticultural grade insecticidal soap. It is safe and is sprayed directly on the problem instead of broadcast over the entire greenhouse.

Green Thumb: Some organic products are very toxic and must be handled with the same degree of caution as synthetic chemicals.

Pests and Beneficial Insects

Beneficials range from the smallest beneficial nematodes all the way up to praying mantises and lizards.

While my greenhouse was being built, I started my seeds in a sunny window of my house. Temperatures were warm and the drainage of the containers was on the poor side, which started a vicious cycle of a fungus gnat problem. Their eggs and larvae live in the soil and the adults fly around being a real nuisance. Fungus gnats feed on mostly on decaying matter, but larvae can also feed on plant roots. The greenhouse was completed shortly thereafter and the plants moved into their new home, and so did the fungus gnats.

The next day I noticed two very tiny spiders took up residence by the plants. My first instinct to get rid of the spiders, as I really dislike spiders, but saw several of the fungus gnats in their webs. Within a couple days, there were no more adults buzzing around the plants. I never saw another one after that! I suspect that the spiders feeding broke the cycle of the adults laying eggs.

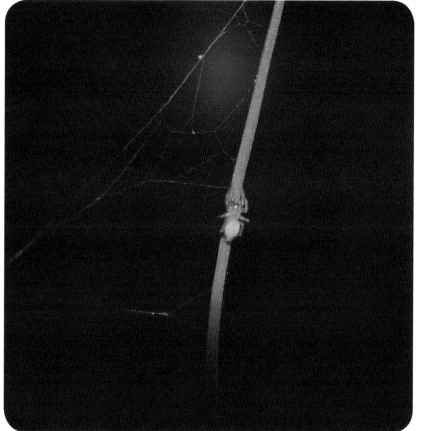

After the spiders irradiated the fungus gnat problem, I have learned to peacefully coexist with my arachnid pest controllers. I will not tolerate a poisonous spider in the greenhouse. In my area, black widows tend to take up residence in manmade structures and in the Midwest the brown recluse can be an issue as well. (Make sure you are able to recognize both.) I keep my gloves in a zippered plastic bag to avoid any surprises!

Spider in the Greenhouse

Nematodes are tiny organisms that live in soil. There are parasitic nematodes that feed on plant roots and beneficial nematodes that feed on all kinds of soil-borne pests. Although usually not a concern for container gardeners since soil is changed out regularly, pests in garden beds can become a real nuisance. If you have a plant failing with no apparent cause, examine the roots. Should there be damage to the root system, have your soil tested for nematodes. Contact your local cooperative extension for a testing source.

Aphids are a gardener's nightmare as they can quickly damage a plant if not caught early. They live on the underside of leaves and the fastest way to be rid of them to blast the leaves with a strong jet of water. Once the aphids fall off, they will not climb back on the plant and die. Insecticidal soap can also be sprayed on the underside of leaves. Make a habit of checking leaves on a regular basis to catch a problem before it starts. So what feeds on aphids? Ladybugs and lacewings! They see a colony of aphids as a veritable buffet.

Whiteflies also feed on the underside of leaves and can be a common nuisance to greenhouse owners. Marigolds emit a chemical that is known to repel whiteflies and they also seem to stay away from basil. Whiteflies are attracted to the color yellow. Yellow sticky traps are effective for catching them. Lacewing larvae are a good predator of whiteflies.

The praying mantis is a very effective predator, however does not discriminate its prey and will eat pests, beneficial insects as well as other praying mantis! I had a praying mantis briefly take up residence in the greenhouse and it ate a couple of my greenhouse spiders before it moved on to "greener pastures". Lizards also dine on insects and tend to love the warm conditions of the greenhouse.

Sealing up your greenhouse goes a long way with keeping pests out. Put screens up over your ventilation intake and exhaust. When my greenhouse first went up, I saw quite a few "little buggies". After sealing up and screening everything, an insect or spider sighting is few and far between.

Young Praying Mantis

So where do you get beneficial insects? They usually just show up where the food is and will move in shortly after pests do. However if the need is great, there are companies that specialize in beneficial insects and you can mail order young insects for release in the greenhouse.

Fertilizing Plants

Good soil gives plants all the nutrients they need. However when we use the same gardening bed over and over, or a plant has lived in a container, human intervention can be necessary to replenish the soil of its lost nutrient value.

How often should we fertilize? Well, that depends. Liquid fertilizers are a quick boost and fade quickly. Granules are slower releasing and applied less frequently. Compost is decomposed organic matter that continues to provide nutrient value as it continues to break down in the soil. Which you use is a matter personal preference.

Plants that receive the nutrients they need are healthy and vibrant.

What do the Numbers Mean?

Fertilizer products that are commercially sold whether synthetic or organic all have a three number system displayed on its label. For example, a package could display 15-10-15. Each number represents a percentage of a particular nutrient. The first number represents nitrogen, the second phosphorus and the third potassium. Why is this important? Each nutrient provides a particular function to the plant.

Nitrogen encourages green, leafy growth. Lawn fertilizer is a good example of a product high in nitrogen. Ever notice how green the grass gets after it is fertilized? (As a side note, high nitrogen synthetic lawn fertilizer can run off with rain water into the storm drains and out to large bodies of water causing a host of trouble for the natural ecosystem.) If the green appears to be fading from plant leaves and slightly yellowing, your plant may be experiencing nitrogen deficiency. Non-flowering ornamental plants benefit from nitrogen to produce lush growth.

Phosphorus encourages flowering and root growth. This nutrient is useful for plants grown solely for their flowers or to encourage edibles to produce blossoms that become fruit and vegetables. If you have flowering plants that are producing all kinds of leaves but no blossoms, there is most likely too much nitrogen or not enough phosphorus in the soil.

Potassium is good for all around plant vigor, encouraging root development, disease resistance and hardiness. An ailing plant would most likely benefit from potassium.

Plants also require secondary nutrients, however not in large amounts. Although they are important, there are oftentimes all ready plentiful in the soil and supplementation is not required. These nutrients are calcium, magnesium and sulfur. The best way to determine if your garden needs these nutrients is to have a soil test through your local Cooperative Extension.

There is such a thing as over fertilizing and doing so can damage your plants. Make sure to follow your package directions. Many potting mixes already come with fertilizers. If you purchase premixed potting medium, check the packaging before adding fertilizer to new mix.

There are several ways to apply fertilizer. How you do it depends on the type of product and whether you are working with just soil, or soil with a plant growing in it.

Green Thumb:

I prefer to use compost or an evenly balanced organic fertilizer. Not only is it less complicated, it provides my plants with a good balance of what they need to grow.

Turning In

When preparing soil, you most likely turn in the fertilizer. It goes just as it sounds. Apply the fertilizer, and then with a garden trowel or shovel, begin turning the soil over in order to mix in the fertilizer product. By amending the soil, your plants' new home will be full of everything that they need to get a good start on life.

Many container gardeners like to add slow-release granules to their potting mix prior to planting container gardens. Since the granules release their nutrients slowly, the plant is fertilized over time instead of all at once.

Side Dressing

Whether in gardening beds or containers, a plant growing in the soil makes turning in no longer possible. To add side dressing to your plants, apply powdered or granule fertilizer to the soil surface around the plant. You may also choose to lightly scratch the surface of the soil in order to encourage the fertilizer into the soil. Then water well and you're done!

Liquid Fertilizer

Liquid fertilizer can be viewed as a quick "pick me up" in the plant world. It is used by plants quickly and then runs out just as fast. It can also potentially leech out of the soil in container plants during regular watering. Liquid fertilizer does have its upside in that a nutrient deficient plant can get what it needs to get healthy again quickly. Two popular organic liquid fertilizers are fish emulsion and liquid seaweed. If you use fish emulsion, make sure to purchase deodorized. Deodorized still has odor, just not as foul.

Compost

Composting makes a big impact on the garden. Compost is inexpensive to make and the rewards to your garden are phenomenal. There is no better cure for poor soil quality than compost! When compost is turned in, poor draining soil drains better and loose soil retains more moisture. The nutrient value of compost is high and plants just love the stuff. Container gardeners can add it to their potting mix and reap the benefits.

Finished compost is decomposed organic matter, also sometimes called humus. Not only are the immediate benefits great, there are other benefits outside the garden as well. Plants will not rely on synthetic fertilizers. Fewer chemicals are added to the environment making their way into water supplies. Garden, lawn and kitchen waste is not making its way into the landfill. And to top it off, composting is easy!

Yes, I love compost.

Green Thumb: Not all plants love nutrient rich garden soil. In the desert southwest, there are a large number of plants that prefer poor soils, so be sure to research your plants' requirements. Plants that are native to desert regions have specific soil requirements.

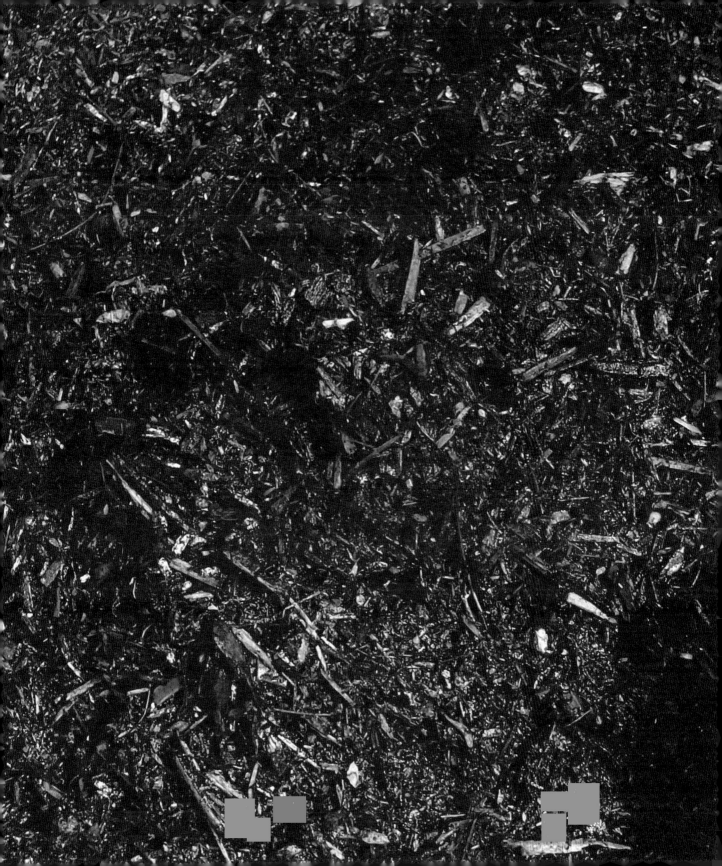

The Compost Pile

The first step to composting is locating a place for the pile. It should be out of view, but not inconvenient. If you can't get to it, you won't use it.

The second step is to contain it. Commercial bins are available or you can build your own. At a minimum, your bin should be three-foot square and three feet high. Any smaller and the pile will not generate and retain heat, which is essential to the decomposition process. A pile's internal temperature can get up to 150 degrees Fahrenheit, so don't be surprised to see steam in the winter. Larger is fine, but not so large that you cannot access the pile.

The compost pile does not need to be complicated. When I was a kid, my dad and I started a compost pile using just poultry wire four feet high and created a four-foot diameter circle held up by stakes.

Currently I live in a very windy area and the bin I have now has a lid on it to keep all the goodies inside. My bin is a two-bin system. One side is for adding new materials and the other is a pile going through the decomposition process. Those with lawns may consider a three-bin system since there is more material going in to the pile.

Compost Materials

So what do you put in a compost pile? Organic materials! Lawn clippings (that are not treated with pesticide), leaves, spent plants and the like. You can also put kitchen waste in the pile, just no meat, dairy or grease as they will attract rodents and may create a pathogen hazard in the pile. Cut up your kitchen waste and crush your eggshells and bury them in the pile. Even coffee grounds with the filters are excellent composting materials. The more the merrier! In fact, Starbucks instituted a program called "Grounds for Your Garden" where you can pick up their used coffee grounds for use in your garden at no charge.

Manure is also an excellent composting material, but be wary of your source. Only use manure from vegetarian animals such as horses and chickens. Carnivorous animal manure can contain pathogens that may not be killed during the composting process.

The recipe for compost success is a 50/50 mix of brown and green materials. Brown materials are dead garden material, sawdust and newspaper. Green materials are manure, kitchen scraps, green plants and coffee grounds. Layer them all together, water once a week (during dry spells) and await compost success. When watering your pile, it should never be soaking wet, just about the consistency of a wrung out sponge. Those living in the desert southwest may need to check on the moisture level more often during the heat of summer. Those living in areas with heavy rainfall may need to cover the bin to prevent too much moisture.

Composting Do's & Don'ts

Do compost organic materials like kitchen scraps and yard waste.

Don't compost lawn clippings treated with pesticide.

Do compost napkins and paper towels.

Don't compost meat and dairy.

Do compost manure from vegetarian animals.

Don't compost manure from carnivorous animals.

Do turn your compost pile to promote good aeration.

Don't let your compost pile dry out or become water logged.

Do bury kitchen waste in the pile to discourage pest problems.

Do locate your compost pile where you will be able to give attention on a weekly basis.

Do spread your finished compost to all your plants!

Running Hot & Cold

The difference between a hot and cold compost pile is merely how often you turn it. Turning the pile means getting in there with a garden fork or cultivator and mixing everything up. Turn and water your pile once a week and you could have finished compost in three months whereas leaving the pile to its own devices could take a year to result in finished compost. One method is not necessarily better than the other, the only difference is the amount of time before compost is ready for the garden.

There are bins on the market that look like metal drums turned on their sides. Compost material is added and the bin is turned with a handle once a day resulting in finished compost much faster. I have not tried one, but heard good things about them.

The Role of Oxygen

The microbes that live in a compost pile require oxygen. It is those microbes that break down the organic material that creates that lovely finished compost. Moisture aids greatly in the composting process, however a soggy pile will not decompose as quickly because the pile is deprived of oxygen (anaerobic). Turning the pile regularly will provide oxygen deep in the pile where all the decomposition magic happens. To turn the pile, use a garden fork or compost aerator and mix the materials in the pile. A compost aerator is a fancy pole that has prongs that collapse when pushed into the pile and expand when pulled out.

Green Thumb: Every time you add materials, make it a habit to turn and water the pile. Good compost habits result in faster finished compost.

Will it Smell?

A good compost pile will not be rank. If your pile has an odor, is attracting flies or is slow to decompose, there is an issue that needs to be addressed. The pile is either too wet or contains too much green material. Add more brown material and turn the pile.

Finished compost smells earthy, is dark brown and has a crumbly consistency. The pile itself will be around one-third its original size and the internal temperature will have dropped. Sift out any large material and add it to the next pile.

Green Thumb: When you add kitchen scraps and the like, make sure to cover them by moving other material over them. This will prevent the pile from attracting flies.

When Trouble Strikes

So you've added all your materials and the pile is not shrinking? It is time to turn in more green material and add water. One of the issues gardeners in the desert southwest experience is hot, dry climate that can quickly dry out a compost pile. Every time I take kitchen scraps out to the compost bin, I fill my scrap container with water not only to rinse it out, but to also add water to the pile. Whenever I turn the pile, I make sure to water it as well.

Compost Tea

To give plants a quick organic fertilizer boost, try some tea! Add some finished compost to a bucket of water, stir daily for a few days, and then serve. Either pour some at the base of the plants or spray it on the plants' leaves for foliar feeding.

Deciding What to Grow Under Glass

Now is the time to decide just what to grow inside the greenhouse! Orchids will have different environmental requirements than overwintering plants, so keep that in mind when planning. Each of us goes in with our own expectations of what will happen in the greenhouse.

This section is a guide to help you with certain considerations of growing under glass. It is not a plant reference book, there are so many of those out there that I instead decided to give you the information that helps you to grow these plants indoors.

While the greenhouse does not have to be dedicated to only one purpose, make sure that whatever you use your greenhouse for that the temperature thresholds lay within the same spectrum for all of your plants. Plan accordingly and make sure that your setup is what will keep all your plants happy.

Landscape

My greenhouse was built shortly after my husband and I moved to a rural area in a house with a graded, empty acre lot. To purchase plants to landscape an acre would put a serious dent in the pocket book, so we turned to the greenhouse as a way to grow plants to use in the landscape. The real pride of my greenhouse is one area is devoted to a tree nursery. Three varieties of mesquite trees grow there in pots, waiting for their moment to move out into the landscape!

Many gardeners use their greenhouse space to start annual flower seeds weeks before the last frost, giving their flowers a great start before being adding them into the outdoor planting beds. Others will start their shrubs and perennial flowers in the greenhouse as a way to save money on plantings.

Should you decide to start perennials to plant outside, make sure that the plants are suited to your hardiness zone, otherwise you could potentially lose the plants in the first frost. Plants that are not hardy to your zone can either be grown as annuals or put in containers to move inside during the wintertime.

Properly selecting plants that are suited your climate will save a lot of heartache. Save yourself the frustration of starting plants only to lose them when they are planted outdoors by thoroughly researching the varieties you would like to grow. Since I live in the desert southwest, growing sweet peas would be difficult because of the extreme heat for the majority of the year and the lack of rainfall, so I would have to supplement quite a bit of water.

Starting annuals to be ready for the spring is easy. Check the last frost for your area in The Old Farmer's Almanac (see Resources for a web address). This is the starting point for all of your planning. Check your seed packet to assist you in planning when to start seeds. Most contain information like "start seeds indoors 2 to 4 weeks before the last frost". This is important because you do not want the young plants to outgrow their temporary home before they are transplanted outside.

Available at most nurseries are empty plant flats with the six cell packs that are excellent for starting transplants. They are inexpensive and work great. Just fill the cells with your favorite seed starting mix, sow the seeds according to the packet specifications and away you go!

My favorite local nursery recycles their plant containers, encouraging patrons to return them for a small cash value. I raid the bin and am able to purchase pots for pennies. Once I clean them up, they are ready to use in the greenhouse for all kinds of landscape and seed starting projects.

The options here are almost endless. Take a look at what you want in the outdoor garden and planting beds, and then look into starting them from seed. What could be more gratifying than looking over a planting bed, knowing that you nurtured and raised each of those plants from seed!

Ornamental Plants

Even if you use your greenhouse for edible plants, consider tucking in a few ornamental plants if only for the pleasure of looking at them. As gardeners, we love plants. Perhaps grow something special that does not grow outside in your region or a favorite plant near to your heart.

Cut Flowers

Sweet Violet
Viola odorata

For those in love with cut flowers, a greenhouse provides a fantastic venue for growing more delicate, frost-tender flowering plants. Many types of flowers can be "forced", or manipulated to flower out of season. With many bulbs, simulating their cooling period and then planting in a greenhouse environment can cause spring flowering bulbs to flower out of season.

Get to know what your plants require to flower and then simulate those conditions. You could be enjoying flowers when others only dream of them. These plants make wonderful gifts for other garden lovers.

Plan your plants according to the conditions that make them bloom and enjoy!

Green Thumb: Cut your flowers when the bloom is at its best. If your flowers wilt during the heat of the day, cut them in the morning when blooms are full.

Parry's Penstemon
Penstemon parryi

Succulents

Cacti fall into the category of succulents. Many gardeners are intimidated by growing cactus. The biggest pitfall gardeners run into is water. Desert cactus requires very little water but do still require water! Most prefer their soil to completely dry out between waterings. Make sure to research the light and temperature requirements of your cactus. Not all cactus want full sun, some of them grow naturally in the shade of other plants. Not all cacti require heat year round. Many of them are from the high desert where temperatures dip below freezing during the winter. Keeping this in mind, there is surely a cactus that you can grow in your greenhouse.

Wear gloves when handling a cactus or you could end up in a prickly situation! Thick gloves help protect your hands. For really spiny cacti, a terry cloth washcloth or towel gently wrapped around your plant will give you further protection.

Golden Barrel Cactus
Echinocactus grusonii

Cactus has very specific soil requirements. Rich potting soil is too far from its native environment and the plant will surely suffer. They require sandy, well draining soil. If you are unsure of what to use, look for cactus potting mix at the nursery.

Succulents are drought-tolerant and come from all different kinds of regions. They are strange and unusual plants and can be quite rewarding to grow. If you had trouble growing them in the past, consider revisiting the idea with a fresh perspective.

Tropical Plants

When referring to plants, the term "tropical" means the plant comes from an area that is frost-free and with temperatures warm enough to support year-round growth. Many tropical plants will die if temperatures go below sixty. This is why tropical plants are popular houseplants. Some varieties of orchids can tolerate temperatures down to the fifties, but just like any plant, it is important to research and know its requirements. For those living in cold climates, greenhouse temperatures are extremely important as a failed heater or a power-outage during the night could spell disaster! This means that a backup heating system should be in place in case of the worst. On the upside, a lush tropical greenhouse is a beautiful sight to behold when there is snow on the ground outside.

Tropical plants are quite stunning and some border on the bizarre! I recently saw a bat plant (Tacca chantrieri) for the first time and was quite taken with its flower covered in what looked like cat whiskers. The chenille plant (Acalypha hispida) is a personal favorite of mine with its flowers that look like pink fuzzy tails.

Epiphytes are another curiosity. Also called "air plants", they do not root in soil. They typically attach themselves in the crooks of trees, but are not parasitic. They draw their moisture from the air or the surface of the plant to which they have attached. Take care of them by misting them regularly.

Bromeliads are popular tropical plants that come in all kinds of shapes and sizes. One bromeliad is found in the produce department, the pineapple! Each bromeliad has its own light requirements, however most prefer bright, indirect light. They are pretty adaptable with temperatures and can withstand cold to fifty degrees.

Orchids have a reputation of being difficult plants to grow. There are many varieties that prove the contrary. The orchid's major requirements are temperature and light. Moth orchids like bright indirect light and temperatures that decrease at night. Vanda orchids prefer tropical, humid conditions. The different varieties of orchids available are almost countless. I suggest investing in a good orchid reference book to guide you along your orchid journey.

Pineapple Plant

Green Thumb: Watch the greenhouse temperature carefully in the wintertime. Tropical plants are extremely sensitive to the cold.

Overwintering Plants

Using a greenhouse to overwinter plants typically means the greenhouse is not heavily heated in the winter, merely kept above freezing. In this cool space, tender plants can be brought in to avoid frost damage. Growth slows during the winter, so watering should be decreased.

It is common to overwinter bulbs in a cold greenhouse, however if you keep your greenhouse warm in the winter, a garage space will usually work just fine for bulbs. When preparing your bulbs, gently dig them up. Cut off the foliage, clean the bulbs off and allow them to air dry for a couple days. Now they are ready to store.

Some plants die back in the winter and go dormant. With these plants, place their containers in the greenhouse and significantly decrease watering until spring.

A greenhouse used to overwinter plants can be quite useful for outdoor container gardeners. Clay pots are notorious for cracking during freezing temperatures if left outdoors with potting mix in them.

Pink Hyacinths

Tulips, Hemisphere

Edibles

Using the greenhouse for food crops really covers two areas, starting the plants in the greenhouse and growing the plants in the greenhouse.

For those with an outdoor kitchen garden or vegetable plot, the greenhouse is a fantastic place to start vegetable seeds. Varieties of vegetable plants at nurseries can be limited, and by starting your own plants from seed, you can grow all sorts of usual and unusual varieties of vegetables. Imagine growing watermelon with yellow flesh instead of red and even sweeter! Or how about a white eggplant? Perhaps some heirloom tomatoes are your love? Starting your own vegetable seeds indoors saves money on plants and also gives you a head start on the growing season since plants can be started before the last frost.

Some indoor gardeners grow their vegetables and herbs under glass. If you live in an area where temperatures and conditions are not ideal for growing outside, the greenhouse definitely has its appeal! The growing season is also much longer and vegetables are protected from birds, rabbits and deer. Although growth slows during the winter, nothing beats a fresh, ripe tomato when the weather outside is cold and blustery.

Out of all the types of plants to grow in the greenhouse, I spend the most time discussing edibles because most of them we grow not for foliage or flowers, but for the tasty treasures they produce. Therefore, more interaction is required from us since we have removed outside influence by growing under glass.

Bush Bean Seedling

Vegetables

We may be tempted to let our plants set fruit whenever they want, but for better plant health, it is often beneficial to pluck the flowers off when the plants are still young and small. This way energy is diverted to growing a healthy plant, then allow it to flower and set fruit when the plant is mature. By allowing a plant to set fruit while still immature, growth can be stunted and productivity reduced.

Most vegetables fit into two categories, warm season and cool season. Although the greenhouse does not have the season extremes like the outdoors, it does still experience its own seasons. The outdoor temperature affects the indoor temperature, even though we intervene to regulate it.

Cool Season Vegetables

Red Sails Lettuce

Here in the Southwest, the cool season is not cool enough in the greenhouse for me to grow peas indoors, but I am able to grow several heat tolerant varieties lettuce. For those in the north, cool season veggies are great because they are protected from below freezing temperatures inside the greenhouse.

Some examples of cool season vegetables are salad greens, peas, onions, potatoes, broccoli, cauliflower, cabbage, spinach, and most root vegetables. Keep in mind though that your greenhouse space is at a premium. Potatoes and onions are inexpensive to purchase at the grocery store and greenhouse space is limited, so perhaps consider planting these outside. If you have the space or just love potatoes and onions, by all means, grow whatever makes you happy!

Broccoli & Cauliflower

Both broccoli and cauliflower require a bit of room to grow, make sure to adequately space the plants. They also need cooler temperatures otherwise the heads can be small and bitter tasting. Both are great to start in the greenhouse and move into the outdoor garden.

Lettuce, Greens and Spinach

Funny thing about plants, they really want to produce seeds! Warmer temperatures encourage lettuce, greens and spinach to bolt and produce seeds. Bolting is when the plant sends up a flower shoot to begin seed production. The downside is the leaves turn bitter and become unpalatable. Look for an area of the greenhouse that stays cooler and is partially shaded.

Grow your lettuce in the cooler months and look for varieties that are heat-tolerant and resist bolting. There are three types of lettuce: loose-leaf, head and Bibb (loose heads). Head lettuce such as iceberg can be difficult to grow in a greenhouse, as they can be very prone to bolting as soon as it gets warm. Some salad greens like radicchio are a bit more tolerant to the heat. I have had great success with Simpson Elite lettuce. It is a loose-leaf lettuce and is very tender with a mild taste.

Simpson Elite Lettuce

Green Thumb: Keep lettuce under the bench in a cooler, semi-shaded area to stave off lettuce bolt as long as possible.

Another avenue to consider is to harvest while the plants are young for baby greens. This is why I prefer loose-leaf varieties because I can snip off leaves to make a salad at dinner without stopping the growth of the plant. Successively sowing your greens is a good idea. Should one batch bolt, move the younger greens into a cooler area of the greenhouse and start harvesting earlier if possible.

Peas

There are some dwarf (bush) cultivars of peas, but most grow on vines three to six feet long with a strong desire to climb. Make sure to provide them with a trellis or series of strings to climb. They can be prolific producers; the more you pick, the more they produce. There are heat-tolerant varieties that are better suited to the sunny, winter greenhouse. Peas are self-pollinating, making them super easy to grow and harvest.

Green Thumb: Peas are a lightweight vine. A simple "teepee" of three bamboo stakes placed over the peas will keep them happy with a place to climb.

Potatoes

Should you decide to grow potatoes in your greenhouse, they can grow in a container with some adaptation. I have seen people use a five-gallon bucket with drainage holes drilled in the bottom. Only fill it a third of the way up with soil when initially planting and as the potatoes grow, keep adding more soil. It is imperative to keep the potato tubers (the part you eat) covered with soil. If exposed to the sun, they will turn green. Yuck! Smaller varieties of potatoes, such as red potatoes, tend to be better suited to growing in a container. You can also harvest potatoes when the tubers are still small for "new potatoes".

Root Vegetables

Root vegetables in containers require a bit of foresight into how big the roots of these vegetables get. Long rooted vegetables like carrots require a deep container to have enough room to grow. Adding a bit of horticultural sand (weed-free washed sand) to your potting mix also helps them grow straight and long since the soil is loose. Short-varieties of carrots are better suited to container life.

Wide rooted vegetables like turnips and beets require wider containers since more space is required in between the plants. There are some cylindrical shaped varieties that require less spacing.

Warm Season Vegetables

In my opinion, it is the warm season vegetables where the greenhouse really shines. The growing season is greatly extended, nighttime temperatures are warmer and it is always a pleasure to eat fresh-off-the-vine produce. Most plants though begin to taper off their productivity when temperatures are over ninety degrees.

Beans

Most of us who have been gardening since we were kids and have fond summer memories of eating snap beans right off the plant. Beans are easy to grow and pretty forgiving. Most varieties do not require pollination and will set fruit on their own. Beans love the warmth but fava beans are an exception and require cool temperatures to be productive.

There are two types of beans, bush and pole. Bush beans grow in a bushy form and pole beans require support, as they are climbers. In fact, if you have a corn growing in the greenhouse, you can use the stalk as a sort of living trellis for pole beans! Semi-dwarf varieties produce a shorter vine if height is an issue.

Harvest beans when the pod fills out. The more you pick, the more the plant produces. If you are growing beans for soups, then allow them to mature and dry on the vine.

Okra

Okra plants love the heat and do not require pollination, making growing them in a warm greenhouse easy. Living in the Southwest, running into other okra lovers is a rarity, but those from the South can definitely appreciate growing your own. Make sure to harvest while the pods are small, otherwise you will end up with some pretty tough okra. Be careful not to over water the okra plants!

Corn

Corn stalks are very tall and the yield is not that high per stalk, so corn may be better suited to your outdoor garden unless you have extra room in the greenhouse. Dwarf varieties are better suited to indoor gardening, however they are not always readily available and a large container will still be required. Even still, corn stalks are fun to grow!

Direct sow corn in the container that will be its home for the duration as it does not take transplanting very well. Once the tassels start to form, pollinate it by shaking the stalks. When it comes time to harvest, corn tastes best when cooked right after pulling the ears off the stalk. The sugar in corn quickly begins to convert to starch after harvest.

Sweet Potatoes

Sweet potato vines can become unruly and quickly take over a space, so grow them up a trellis. They are ready to harvest in about four months. Harvest by gently digging around the plant to lift the tubers.

Cucumbers

Cucumbers plants can be a bit finicky about their growing conditions, but are easy to grow provided the right variety is selected and a watchful eye is kept on their environment. Some varieties require pollination and others do not. When buying seeds, look for varieties suited to greenhouse production and do not require pollination. I have had great luck with the variety "Sweet Success". If the flowers are left un-pollinated, the cucumbers produced are seedless. And they are very flavorful! I recommend training the vine up a string to save space and make harvesting easy.

Check the seed packet to find the ideal size of cucumbers for harvest. When left to grow too large, they loose a lot of their tenderness and tastiness. I remember when I was a kid the time I picked a cucumber that must have been two feet long! Even though I was excited about my gigantic vegetable find, it tasted terrible.

Also note that cucumber plants will not tolerate the cold. Production will slow and the plant will eventually die if the temperatures drop below sixty degrees. They are also susceptible to fungus and mildew, so water only at the base of the plant and be careful to not allow water to splash on the leaves.

Eggplant

Growing eggplant has nearly the same condition requirements as growing cucumbers. Eggplant do not like an excess of water, so make sure the drainage is good and carefully monitor the soil moisture so you do not over water the plants. Most eggplants also require a long growing season. Eggplant does require pollination and is best achieved by transferring pollen with a soft-bristled artist brush.

There are some really fantastic varieties of eggplant ranging all kinds of colors and shapes that you do not see in the grocery store. Just another joy of growing from seed!

Peppers

Peppers fall into two categories, sweet and hot. Both have a bushy growing habit. They can cross-pollinate, so keep them on opposite sides of the greenhouse if you grow both. Imagine the surprise of biting into a sweet pepper that is spicy!

These plants can be particular about their temperature. Too low and production slows down. Too hot fruit does not set. To add to it, when the plant becomes stressed (either from water or temperature), it experiences leaf drop. Given the right conditions, pollination is easy. Just tap the flowers and then wait for peppers! With sweet peppers, they can either be picked at the green stage or allowed to mature and change colors. If you are saving seeds for growing, the pepper will need to be allowed to mature on the plant to produce viable seeds.

Squash

Summer squash (including zucchini) is named thusly so because it is harvested while the squash is young and immature. Most grow in a bush form and require pollination. A few zucchini varieties do not require pollination, but that should be noted in the seed catalog. Winter squash are harvested mature, and therefore require a lot more time on the plant. Most winter squash grow on vines and require a lot of trellis space.

Tomatoes

For most vegetable gardeners, tomatoes are the real gems of the greenhouse. Store-bought tomatoes pale in comparison to the flavor of a perfectly ripe tomato right off the vine. Growing tomatoes in the greenhouse is not too different from growing tomatoes outside, with a few extra considerations.

When transplanting tomato seedlings, whether to a garden bed or container, strip back the leaves on the lower half and then plant it at a depth halfway up the stem. I know this goes against the normal transplanting convention. The part of the plant that is underground will grow roots from the stem, giving the plant a strong root structure for more vigorous plant growth.

Tomato plants require pollination. As discussed in the pollination chapter, tapping the support stake can pollinate tomatoes however my best tomato pollination success is by holding a vibrating toothbrush against the blossom.

Tomatoes require regular watering. Irregular watering habits can cause misshaped tomatoes, and over watering can cause leaf curl.

Temperature plays a big part in tomato production. Lower than fifty degrees or higher than ninety degrees and fruit will not regularly set.

Grape Tomatoes

When selecting your varieties of tomato plants, take note as to whether they are determinate or indeterminate. Determinate varieties grow in a compact bushy form and rarely require more than a support stake. Indeterminate varieties will require extra support methods.

It may be tempting to purchase starter tomato plants from the nursery, but I highly recommend starting your plants with seed. Choose varieties with disease resistance. In tight quarters and high humidity, disease can spread quickly. Also, if you have trouble growing a particular variety of tomatoes, try another. Roma tomato plants just do not grow well in my greenhouse, but I heard of other greenhouse gardeners that have great success with them. However the grape tomato variety "Jelly Bean" produces like crazy in my space. Just like any gardening project, if something does not grow well, try something else!

Fruits

Growing fruit in a greenhouse has its pros and cons. On the upside, fruit is sheltered from birds and pests. On the downside, most fruit grows on a tree and takes up a lot of space, as they can get very tall. Most fruit trees require a certain number of cold hours per year. Many fruit trees require a second tree to cross-pollinate. Some fruit trees do not require pollination, like a select few varieties of figs. Check the seed catalog before embarking on a greenhouse fruit tree. Look for dwarf varieties than can be grown in containers and do not require pollination. Varieties that produce fruit without pollination are called parthenocarpic.

Fruit that grows on small plants and bushes may be easier to manage. As always, check its pollination requirements.

Strawberries

I have had no luck growing strawberries from seed, so I buy mine as bare roots in the late winter. The plants themselves do well in the greenhouse and produce fruit easily. Strawberries are in season during the summer. They are pollinated simply by gently rubbing an artist brush over the center of the flower. Even pollination ensures nicely shaped fruits. Misshapen fruits are oftentimes the result of uneven pollination.

Strawberries are available as June bearing and ever-bearing. June bearing produce one large crop of strawberries while ever bearing produce several smaller crops. Day neutral varieties produce throughout the season. Most strawberry production is dependent upon the number of hours of sunlight per day, while the day neutral varieties do not. Day neutral, ever bearing varieties will most likely be your choice for greenhouse production.

Ozark Beauty Strawberries

Other Types of Berries

Definitely do your research with berries. Dwarf varieties are better suited to containers. The plants will likely do better outside the greenhouse, as many types require a cold dormancy period during the winter.

Melons

Melons require a long, warm growing season to produce. They also require pollination by inserting the male flower into the female flower. The female flowers are easily recognizable with their small, immature fruit behind the flower.

Grow melon vines up a trellis to save space, but fashion slings for the fruit so they do not pull themselves off the vine before they are ripe. Look for dwarf varieties with short vines and smaller fruits.

Green Thumb:

Select varieties of melon vines that produce smaller fruit, around two to four pounds, to save space. A couple of my favorite melon varieties are Earlidew Honeydew and Lil' Sweet Cantaloupes. Both produce small melons that pack a lot of taste power into a tiny little package.

Check your seed catalogs for dwarf melons that are recommended for containers and are prolific producers.

The honeydew melon will change from green to golden when ripe.

Cantaloupes will easily slip from the stem when they are ready to harvest.

The most common method to test when watermelon is ripe is to tap the fruit and listen for a hollow sound. The other is to look at the underside of the melon. When it changes from white to a cream color, it is ready to harvest.

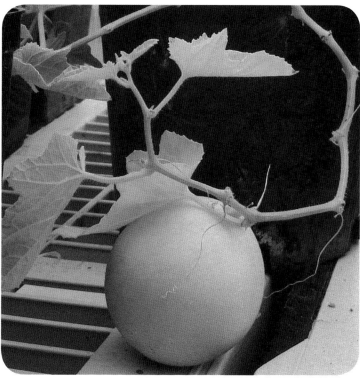

Earlidew Honeydew Melon

Herbs

Herbs are not only popular for their culinary value, they are easy to grow. Edible flowers are also regaining popularity. A favorite of many gardeners is the nasturtium flower with its peppery tasting flowers. Edible flowers make great salad garnishes. Entire books have been devoted to growing herbs, so I will name a few popular ones here as well as the ones that require a little special attention. Many popular herbs are native to the Mediterranean and require warm conditions and infrequent watering. With a greenhouse, we can better control the conditions for our plants. Areas with a lot of

Genovese Basil, Parsley and Mint

Sweet Basil

Basil

Basil is a perennial herb if protected from frost. It is quite sensitive to below freezing temperatures and thrives in hot conditions with well-draining soil. This is a great greenhouse herb, but should be pinched out once it reaches four sets of leaves on the main stem. This will encourage a bushier growing habit and production of more leaves, which is why we grow basil in the first place!

When we say "basil", we are typically referring to Sweet Basil. There is a whole world of basil to explore! Open any seed catalog and you will see all the amazing varieties available. Genovese Basil is very popular in Italian cooking and is a prolific producer of leaves. There are also basils with hints of other flavors and scents such as lemon, lime, licorice or cinnamon. Opal basil has deep purple foliage. So many plants, so little time…

Dill

Dill is also an annual herb with a long taproot, but will reseed like crazy if given the chance. It should also not be planted next to fennel as it can cross-pollinate easily.

Chives

Chives are one of my favorite herbs to grow. They are so easy and again, suited to containers and the greenhouse environment. They are members of the onion family and the hollow spiky leaves have a mild onion flavor. Chives produce purple "pom-pom" flowers that are also edible. There are garlic chives with a hint of garlic flavor. Garlic chives are a bit more sensitive to the heat and could go dormant in the summertime if temperatures get too high.

When growing outside, the leaves die back in the winter. In my greenhouse, chives stay green all year round!

Cilantro

Cilantro leaves are very popular in Mexican salsa and have a very distinct flavor. It is best to direct sow cilantro as it has a long taproot that does not take to transplanting very well. It is an annual and short-lived, so start new plants when old ones start to decline.

Common Chives

Mint

Mint is extremely easy to grow if not neglected of water. If you have never grown mint before, be forewarned that it can quickly take over a space! I highly recommend growing it in a container even in you use planter beds in your greenhouse. When I lived in the Midwest, we grew mint in one planter on the side of the house. It took over the entire bed and no matter how many times we pulled it up it kept coming back. When kept under control, it is a very rewarding plant to grow.

Rosemary

Rosemary is a very tough, rugged plant and easy to grow, starting it from seed is not so simple. For your best chances, the seeds must be very fresh and even still the germination rate can be low. Once I sowed an entire packet of seeds and had one seed germinate five weeks later! These types of plants are more successfully propagated with cuttings. If you must propagate from seed, make sure your seed is really fresh and obtained from a source that guarantees a good germination rate. Germination occurs in full sun and in slightly cooler temperatures, around sixty degrees. Make sure your potting mix drains well and is a bit on the alkaline side for rosemary to really thrive.

I enjoy experimenting with herbs. I love to make marinades for meats using olive oil and a handful of herbs. The flavors are always a welcome surprise every time I try a new combination. The addition of lime or lemon juice creates a whole different set of flavors.

Mint Leaves

Green Thumb:

Whatever reason you choose to use your herbs, grow your favorites and try varieties that you cannot get in stores. Be adventurous!

Life in the Greenhouse

The greenhouse can be a labor of love, yet the rewards are endless. Not everything will go right the first time, but as gardeners, we experiment. Try not to get discouraged and if something goes wrong, look at it as an opportunity to try something new. As gardeners, we learn from our mistakes. When it goes right, it feels that much better knowing that you were the one that made the conditions optimal for your plants.

With dedication and a passion for plants, a greenhouse provides a creative outlet and an amazing space to nurture not only your plants, but yourself as well.

Get out there and grow!

Resources

Cooperative Extensions

In the United States, the Cooperative Extension Service is a division of the US Department of Agriculture. Cooperative Extensions are a public education program offered to each state as an outreach service educating in the areas of agriculture, health, family, 4-H and economic development.

Each Cooperative Extension also offers its services of Master Gardeners, to provide information regarding gardening in their respective region. The Master Gardeners volunteer out in the community to educate the public and answer gardening questions. Many county extension offices offer demonstration gardens.

For more information regarding the Cooperative State Research, Education and Extension Service, visit http://www.csrees.usda.gov/

Useful Websites

The web is a fantastic tool for gathering information. These are just a few site suggestions for the greenhouse gardener.

Growing Under Glass

http://www.growingunderglass.com
The author's greenhouse website and blog.

ACF Greenhouse Exhaust Fans & CFM Calculator

http://www.littlegreenhouse.com/fan-calc.shtml
Online tools provided by ACF Greenhouses to calculate the size of ventilation fan needed based on the size of your greenhouse.

Charley's Greenhouse & Garden

http://www.charleysgreenhouse.com/
Online catalog of greenhouses and greenhouse accessories.

Flowers of India

http://www.flowersofindia.net/
Offers a fantastic section of understanding botanical names.

Garden Web

http://www.gardenweb.com/
Presented by iVillage, a large online forum with many subjects related to gardening. Also includes a special greenhouse forum.

The Old Farmer's Almanac

http://www.almanac.com/garden/frostus.php
Last frost dates in the United States.

PlantFiles on Dave's Garden

http://www.davesgarden.com/guides/pf/
A fantastic tool for getting technical information on plants such as temperature, water and soil requirements.

The Seed Site

http://theseedsite.co.uk/
This site has an abundance of information about seeds, growing seeds and botanical names.

Starbucks Coffee Company: Grounds for Your Garden

http://www.starbucks.com/aboutus/compost.asp
Information regarding the Starbucks composting program. Pick up used coffee grounds for free from your local Starbucks to use your compost pile.

USDA Plant Hardiness Zone Map

http://www.usna.usda.gov/Hardzone/
Find your hardiness zone to assist in selecting plant suitable to your region's low temperatures.

Sources of Beneficial Insects

There are numerous companies specializing in the sale of beneficial insects. Make sure the company you order from carries a good replacement policy should your insects not make the mail order trip. There are also regulations about insects crossing state and country borders. Be educated on your area's laws and contact your local cooperative extension or insect source for guidance.

The Beneficial Insect Co.
PO Box 119
Glendale Springs, NC 28629
Telephone: 1-336-973-8490
http://www.thebeneficialinsectco.com/

The Bug Factory, Ltd.
1636 E. Island Highway
Nanoose Bay, British Columbia
V9P 9A5
http://www.thebugfactory.ca/

Seed Catalogs

Although seed packets are available seasonally through nurseries and discount stores, they typically only offer a narrow selection of plant varieties. When you are looking for something special, take a look a seed catalog. I have included a few of my favorites here, however entering "seed catalog" in an internet search engine will yield a plethora of sites.

The Cooks' Garden
PO Box C5030
Warminster, PA 18974
Telephone: 1-800-457-9703
http://www.cooksgarden.com/

Gurney's Seed & Nursery Co.
P.O. Box 4178
Greendale, IN 47025-4178
Telephone: (513) 354-1491
http://www.gurneys.com/

Johnny's Selected Seeds
955 Benton Avenue
Winslow, Maine 04901
Telephone: 1-877-564-6697
http://www.johnnyseeds.com/

Park Seed Company
1 Parkton Ave
Greenwood, SC 29647
Telephone: 1-800-213-0076
http://www.parkseed.com/

Seeds of Change
Telephone: 1-888-762-7333
http://www.seedsofchange.com/

Seedman.com
3421 Bream St.
Gautier, MS 39553
http://www.seedman.com/

Sheffield's Seed Company
269 Auburn Road, Route 34
Locke, New York 13092
Telephone: (315) 497-1058
http://www.sheffields.com/

Stokes Seeds
PO Box 548
Buffalo, New York 14240-0548
Telephone: 1-716-695-6980
http://www.stokeseeds.com/

Swallowtail Garden Seeds
122 Calistoga Road, #178
Santa Rosa, CA 95409
Telephone: 1-707-538-3585
http://www.swallowtailgardenseeds.com/

Thompson & Morgan
220 Faraday Avenue
Jackson, NJ 08527-5073
Telephone: 1-800-274-7333
http://www.tmseeds.com/

Garden Journal Samples

Environmental Journaling

At the start of each month, note the temperature inside, outside and any changes you have made to the greenhouse environment such as heaters and shade cloths.

Month	Min/Max Temperature Inside	Min/Max Temperature Outside
January		
February		
March		
April		
May		
June		
July		
August		
September		
October		
November		
December		

Plant Journaling

Each plant you choose to grow should be well documented for future reference. By documenting how you grew the plant and whether it succeeded or failed, your journal will assist you in growing future plants of the same variety.

Common Name	
Botanical Name	
Source	
Sowed	
Germination	
Transplanted	
Bloom	
Harvest	
Decline	
Notes	

Planning

Wintertime is a great time for planning since plant growth slows down. While looking through seed catalogs, books and magazines, jot down your ideas for the next growing season.

Common Name	Botanical Name	Publication Title	Pg. #

Index

Hilery Hixon lives in Southern Nevada with her husband, Adem. Her Jack Russell Terrier, Jasmine ventures to the greenhouse each morning to assist in the daily activities. She also shares her home with two cats, Hero and Sophia.